AN INTRODUCTION TO

UNIVERSITY LIBRARY

ADMINISTRATION

Frontispiece: Nottingham University Library.

AN INTRODUCTION TO
UNIVERSITY LIBRARY
ADMINISTRATION

(SECOND EDITION, REVISED)

JAMES THOMPSON
BA FLA
Librarian, University of Reading

CLIVE BINGLEY LONDON

FIRST PUBLISHED 1970

THIS REVISED EDITION PUBLISHED 1974 BY CLIVE BINGLEY LTD
16 PEMBRIDGE ROAD LONDON W11
SET IN 10 ON 13 POINT LINOTYPE PLANTIN
AND PRINTED IN GREAT BRITAIN BY THE CENTRAL PRESS (ABERDEEN) LTD
COPYRIGHT © JAMES THOMPSON 1974
ALL RIGHTS RESERVED
0 85157 171 9

By the same author
BOOKS: an anthology (Anne Bingley)
ENGLISH STUDIES: A GUIDE FOR LIBRARIANS

CONTENTS

1*

LIST OF ILLUSTRATIONS

PREFACE TO SECOND EDITION

THE SECTIONS of this book on finance, undergraduate collections, decentralization, little-used materials, computerization, subject specialization and new media have been rewritten for the second edition, and the text as a whole has been updated and augmented where necessary. The list of references, while remaining highly selective, has also been augmented; and four new illustrations have been incorporated.

The author wishes to thank Trent Concrete Limited for supplying the photograph of Nottingham University Library; Mr R F Eatwell for that of Surrey University Library's book issue system; Mr R O MacKenna for that of Glasgow University Library's old and new buildings; the ESL Bristol Group of Companies for that of the Surrey tape-slide carrel; and Memorex UK Ltd for that of the COM catalogue. The rest of the photographs in this book are the work of the University Photographic Department at Reading.

JAMES THOMPSON

I

THE CONTEXT OF A UNIVERSITY LIBRARY

NATIONAL CONTEXT: The last ten years have witnessed the growth of an intense public interest in university affairs. In the early sixties there was the excitement and goodwill generated by the establishment of no fewer than seven new universities (Sussex, East Anglia, York, Essex, Kent, Warwick and Lancaster); in the middle and late sixties, however, a more critical attitude developed, as newspapers and television focused attention on the long series of student protests which began at that time.

Universities will remain of public interest now, because they are almost wholly supported by taxpayers' money. Government expenditure on universities is in the region of three hundred million pounds per annum. The total university student population, which was already 235,250 in 1970/71, is expected to rise to about 320,000 in 1976/77. Universities therefore represent a massive investment by the nation, and are expected to yield a vitally important return in trained and educated manpower.

It is not surprising therefore that in January 1967 the Public Accounts Committee recommended in its report *Parliament and control of university expenditure* (House of Commons Paper 290) that universities should allow their books and records to be inspected by the Comptroller and Auditor General. The Secretary of State for Education and Science told the House of Commons in July 1967 that the ' existence of an independent check on how the universities spend public money should serve to reassure Parliament and the public '. Since January 1 1968 it has therefore become a condition of grant to universities that they permit such an inspection.

However, it has also long been recognized that there should exist an independent body, to act as a buffer between the government and the universities, interpreting the one to the other, and enabling public funds to flow into the universities without direct government intervention. In this way it is possible to reconcile the interests of the state as paymaster and the requirements of national policy, with the proper academic freedom and autonomy of the universities. For fifty years such has been the function of the University Grants Committee, which was established by the issue of a Treasury Minute in July 1919. The UGC's terms of reference, extended in 1946, read: ' To enquire into the financial needs of university education in Great Britain; to advise the Government as to the application of any grants made by Parliament towards meeting them; to collect, examine, and make available information relating to university education throughout the United Kingdom; and to assist, in consultation with the universities and other bodies concerned, the preparation and execution of such plans for the development of the universities as may from time to time be required in order to ensure that they are fully adequate to national needs '.

Universities have been subject to other kinds of change in addition to those brought about by public and government interest. One outcome of the student protests mentioned earlier has been a growing participation by students in university government: whereas in 1966 there were no students on any university Senate, in 1967 there was one with student representation, in 1968 there were six, and by 1970 the number of Senates with student members was fourteen. C K Balmforth, M W Grose and A E Jeffreys, in their article in *Interface* (edited by Balmforth and N S M Cox) mention three further major internal changes. Firstly, teaching methods nowadays incline more towards the intimate and informal guidance provided by seminars and tutorials, rather than the remote delivery of knowledge in the form of set lectures. Secondly, university students are no longer drawn solely from the privileged few; the high proportion of first generation students has been a liberating influence on the university ethos. And thirdly, the academic curriculum has been altered in emphasis and widened in range: classics, as it were, retreat in the face of social sciences.

FUNCTIONS
It is against such a background that the functions of a university library must be seen. A university library is no longer part of an ivory

tower world; it is a practical, service institution, accountable for every aspect of its performance. M A Gelfand in his book *University libraries for developing countries* states: 'The fundamental role of the library is educational. It should not be operated as a mere storehouse of books attached to a reading-room, but as a dynamic instrument of education'.

Gelfand is here summarizing what have elsewhere (Herbert Goldhor in his article on *Some thoughts on the curriculum of library schools;* Harold Lancour in *Training for librarianship in North America;* and P Havard-Williams in *The teaching function of the university library*) been characterized as the three stages of library development. The first of these stages was the *storehouse* period of librarianship: libraries as warehouses, containing books 'carefully stored for indefinite preservation' (Lancour's words). It followed from this that the librarian's role was that of an avid collector and a jealous preserver; actual use of the materials militated against preservation and was therefore discouraged. The second stage of library development is the *service* period: here the criterion is the greatest use of library materials by the greatest number of people. To encourage such use, catalogues and bibliographies are compiled, classification systems devised, circulation systems designed. It is at this stage that practically all libraries have arrived. But now we are moving into the third period of development, where the emphasis is on the *educational function* of the library. Lancour describes the objective of this third stage as 'the creation of a broad and positive form of education, designed for the recognized potential users of the library and which makes use of the materials and services peculiar to the library'.

Robert S Taylor, in his book *The making of a library*, traces the evolutionary progress of academic libraries in a similar, but rather more vivid fashion: 'The cultural surround of libraries has been humanistic and scholarly, and conservative by necessity. This has in the past century been overlain by two attitudes: technical and democratic. The technical approach (or technician when translated to people) grew out of Melvil Dewey's efforts in the 1870's and 1880's and gave the library, as a collection of books, a more efficient set of processes, systems, and organization. Present-day efforts to automate library routines are in this tradition. The democratic approach is a reflection of mid and late-nineteenth century culture and basically grew from the growth and influence of the public library. The development of reference services and readers' advisory services follows this line. Today's efforts, reflecting the democratization of education and the incandescence of media culture, bear the seed for major alteration of the library's goals, functions, and organization. As major molders of the academic library, the faculty, if they give any real thought to it, see the library only in context of the traditional view that the library is for scholarly purposes and wears a sort of halo, standing for humanism because somehow books and reading are humanistic. To pursue the analogy librarians, with some noble exceptions, are in the technical tradition concerned more with objects that come in the back door than with people who may or may not come in the front door. These two elements make up the conventional, and usual, image of the library. Until the third element, the users, are truly incorporated into this picture, and are not merely suppliants, the library will remain but a sophisticated and efficient warehouse '.

The developments described above did not go unnoticed in the Parry Report (officially, the University Grants Committee *Report of the Committee on Libraries*). The Committee commented: 'In the period since the war the most fundamental change in attitude in university libraries has been from the inward-looking conservative method to an outward-looking organization geared more directly to the needs of readers '.

Hand-in-hand with this new and active realization of the purpose of university libraries has come a truer assessment of their importance in the life of universities. The classic statement of the position, and one which has deservedly been quoted again and again, is that made by the University Grants Committee in 1921: 'The character and efficiency of a university may be gauged by its treatment of its central organ—the library'. In essence this was repeated in the paper on *The university library* produced by the Association of University Teachers (September 1964): 'It must be recognized once and for all that university libraries provide an absolutely fundamental service which affects the whole of the university and without which it would cease to function as a centre for teaching and research '.

This same paper defines the role of a university library precisely: ' The prime function of a university library is to provide facilities for study and research for the members of its own institution '. Such a definition does not deny that a university library also has a duty, though secondary, to its local community: to members of other local institutions of higher education, to government organizations, to non-profit-making bodies. It is merely stating priorities. A university library provides the books and journals (not to mention the slides, maps, gramophone records, tapes, theses, films, and microforms) needed by the staff and students of its own university; it processes these materials so that they are usable and retrievable—recording, arranging, maintaining; and it creates the amenities for their use—adequate accommodation, liberal hours of opening and services such as photo-copying.

Nigel Cox in his paper in *Interface* on management criteria in the design of systems for academic libraries makes a useful attempt to analyse further the functions of a university library, under five headings: namely, *control, archive, service, co-operation* and *research and development*. *Control* covers ordering, accessioning, cataloguing, circulation, stocktaking; *archive* is building up the necessary collections; *service* is the professional guidance and assistance offered to users; *co-operation* is the need to link with and contribute to the local and national network of library resources; and *research and development* is the library staff's activity in perfecting the techniques of librarianship. Paul Buck in *Libraries and universities* breaks down the functions in an almost identical way: resources (that is, *archive*), retrieval of information (that is, *control* and *service*), co-ordination (or *co-operation*), and staff capability (*research and development*). But he summarises them effectively and sufficiently in one word, not five. The word he chooses is an almost self-explanatory one: respon-siveness—the alertness and flexibility required to respond to the needs of the university which the library serves.

GOVERNMENT

In serving its university, the university library has to operate within the governing framework of that institution. University policy divides into three main areas: academic policy, financial policy, and planning and building policy. The first of these is the concern of the senate, the principal academic body, which is composed mainly of the university's professors (though most senates now include a wider range of representation). The last two, in general terms, are the concern of the council, the executive body of the university, which is made up mainly of representatives from the locality.

The university library is normally governed by a library committee. This committee may be either a senate committee, or a joint committee of senate and council. In either case it reports to senate. Its function basically is the guardianship of the library: to see that it is well maintained, to frame rules for its use, to guide and promote its further development, and to recommend and secure the necessary finances. These, of course, are also the functions of the university librarian; and, as Woledge and Page remark in *A manual of university and college library practice*, if the librarian has shown himself to be a capable administrator, the library committee's role will be an advisory, supporting, and endorsing, rather than an executive, one: ' enabling the librarian to elaborate his plans in the light of detailed criticism, and in enlisting on behalf of the library a body of enlightened opinion within the university '.

As far as it is possible to do so within a committee which must necessarily be limited in size if it is to be at all workable, membership of the library committee tries usually to reflect the subject and faculty balance of the university. Student representation on it is now common. The academic staff members of the committee should certainly include a sprinkling of the more high-powered university figures—deans and senior professors; the vice-chancellor or deputy vice-chancellor is commonly an *ex officio* member. The obvious advantage of having such members is that the library thereby enlists some influential voices in promoting its aims. The total size of the committee tends to be in the region of a dozen or so.

The university librarian normally acts as secretary to the library committee, and brings his deputy librarian to its meetings with him. There is not a great deal to be said for involving other members of the library staff; for one thing, such membership would unbalance the composition of the committee, the chief merit of which after all is that it represents an outside control on and interest in the affairs of the library. The library staff will already have, or should have, ample scope within the library's ordinary organizational structure to express their views on its running and policy. An additional reason is the need for the university librarian to present a single official library view in public, not (as could happen) a set of contradictory and discordant ' library ' opinions which would only serve (especially if they were on technical matters) to bewilder the lay members of the committee. The deputy librarian, however, has a specific and valuable role to play. First of all, he usually acts as minute-taker, because the university librarian is too actively involved in the committee's discussions to be able at the same time to record its deliberations. And secondly, since the deputy librarian is more closely involved in the day-to-day running of the library, he can be consulted on the precise details of various transactions and routines. These two functions together—that is, of recording the minutes and of providing precise information—tend to prevent the deputy librarian from joining fully in the committee's discussions; but since the university librarian and the deputy librarian work closely together anyway—in the actual preparation of business for the library committee, for instance—this fact is not too important.

What the university librarian brings as business to the meetings of the library committee varies from library to library. Some matters, plainly, are common to all. One is the annual report of the library. The library committee is expected to present to the university (first to senate, and then from senate to council) a yearly account of the library's activities. This document is written by the university librarian, and approved (or amended) by the library committee. The annual report of any library has its own individual style: but the components are basically the same. First there is an introductory paragraph or paragraphs which, as it were, establish the character of the year under review: exceptional pressure on resources; new accommodation, or impending total inadequacy of accommodation; the receipt of some munificent and gratifying gift; staff troubles. This is followed by sections on: additions to stock (books—both purchases and gifts; periodicals; manuscripts, archives; and other types of material); processing operations (cataloguing and binding statistics, for example); services (loans, inter-library loans; statistics of photographic work; stocktaking returns); buildings and equipment; branch libraries and departmental libraries; and staff resignations and appointments.

The report as a whole is finally summed up in the form of a statistical table.

Other standard items of library committee business are the annual and quinquennial library estimates (see the section following, on *Finance*). These are compiled by the university librarian, approved (or amended) by the committee, and transmitted by the librarian to the Vice-Chancellor for consideration by the various university planning and finance committees. Equally standard is the follow-up to the library estimates: the annual allocation of the money which in fact was provided by the university in answer to the estimates—needless to say, there is usually little connection between what was asked for and what is granted. It is the duty of the librarian to allocate wisely such finances as he is given; and it is a function of the library committee—perhaps its most important function—to advise and help the librarian with this work of allocation, and finally to approve it. This particular area of library committee business also points up one of the vital elements in the committee's role: namely, that of supporting the librarian in his decisions. Anything to do with the allocation of funds within a university is a delicate business; on his own, the librarian would often find it difficult to convince each academic department as to the equity and wisdom of such allocations; however, when such allocations have the authority of the library committee behind them, subsequent wrangling tends to be reduced, or if not reduced, at least partly deflected away from the librarian. There is one university librarian in Britain who found himself on appointment without an already-existing library committee; he very quickly arranged to have one, mainly to provide himself with a shield.

A library committee also concerns itself with appointments to the library staff (see chapter III); has reported to it such matters as gifts; and discusses issues such as borrowing regulations (which can be very complicated in an academic library, because of the wide range in the status of users). From time to time, isolated major topics present themselves; perhaps, the setting-up of a library bindery; or a scheme to preserve the university's archives; or the provision of an entirely new service such as a documentation centre. Here, and especially when the project would involve the university organisationally or financially to a considerable extent, the library committee forwards a report, with recommendations, to the senate or to the appropriate university committee. Also from time to time, the library committee has referred to it business by another university body or official: for example, the vice-chancellor might ask the library committee to consider adding student representatives to its membership.

Quite apart from its role of trusteeship, and quite apart from the formal backing it gives to the librarian's decisions, it will be seen that the library committee can act most effectively as a sympathetic forum in which the librarian can examine his problems and test his ideas. Very rarely does a library committee resort to voting procedure; very rarely does it over-ride the librarian's expert and professional recommendations. More often it enables him to formulate and improve his plans, and so inform and sharpen his own performance.

FINANCE

Earlier in this chapter it was noted that government expenditure on universities is of the order of three hundred million pounds per annum. Though some university money does come from endowments and appeals, it is not a significant amount in comparison with that which comes from the government, through the University Grants Committee.

The University Grants Committee prepares the case to the government periodically for the overall financial needs of the universities, after examining the universities' own estimates and proposals. Though the government decides the total sums to be made available, it is the UGC which allocates them between the individual universities. The money provided by the government falls under three headings: recurrent grants, non-recurrent grants and equipment grants. Recurrent grants are determined for periods of five years, and distributed to individual universities as annual sums by the UGC. Non-recurrent grants, to cover building work, the purchase of sites and properties, the payment of professional fees and the furnishing of buildings, are made on an annual basis, as are equipment grants (which, however, universities may accumulate in an equipment fund).

The ordinary needs of a university library are met from its parent institution's recurrent grant. The UGC normally gives recurrent grants as block grants, with no stipulations as to their precise disposition. Thus what a university library receives is decided, not by the UGC, but by its own institution. The annual expenditure of a middle-range British university (4,500-5,000 students) is in the region of five million pounds; and on average 4 percent of this is spent on its library. However, as examination of *Statistics of education* will reveal, this percentage figure of total university expenditure devoted to libraries does vary considerably between institutions according to age and size; in 1968-69, for example, while Birmingham University Library received only 2·2 percent, Warwick received 7·1 percent.

The University Grants Committee's *Report of the Committee on Libraries* of 1967 maintained that the annual cost of library provision in a university of medium size should not fall below 'about 6 percent of the budget of such a university', and since that time British university librarians have pressed for the general adoption of this as a minimum standard, though without much success. Their failure to do so has nothing to do with any lack of determination on their part, nor is it any reflection on their powers of advocacy. The hard realities of a librarian's position in a university context are plainly described by an American university administrator, Robert F Munn, in his article *The bottomless pit, or the academic library as viewed from the Administration Building.* Munn begins by saying that it is certainly the case that 'librarians worry vastly more about the high cost of libraries than do administrators', since most American universities allocate only perhaps 4 or 5 percent of their operating budget to the library, a relatively small and remarkably consistent percentage. He points out that the barriers to a library receiving a higher percentage of university income are three: first, the library is seen as a bottomless pit, being infinitely expandable, and therefore always in pursuit of 'an undefined and presumably unattainable goal'; second, the library cannot exert pressure; and third, nobody has yet succeeded in making a cost-benefit analysis of the contribution of a library to its university. Hence the percentage of university income devoted to library purposes tends to stick at its traditional level.

H F Dammers in his article in *Interface* presents tentative statistics relating to the current operations of British university libraries, and gives a break-down of the budget of the 'average' British university library in percentages, as follows:

Salaries	50%
Books	25%
Periodicals	13%
Binding	6%
Sundries	6%

Little explanation is needed concerning the salaries bill, since this percentage of expenditure on it is well-nigh standard; but it is worth noting that the larger a library becomes, the more noticeably the payroll begins to outstrip the bookfund. Indeed, Rogers and Weber in the context of American university libraries, give 60 percent as the normal. Similarly, it is obvious that a proportion of a library's budget must go on binding, and it is generally conceded that this national figure of 6 percent is too low; the Standing Conference of National and University Libraries, for example, in the model annual budget prepared for the Parry Committee, recommended a figure of 25 percent of the grant for books and periodicals. The sum for Sundries merely covers such standard items as stationery, minor office equipment, travel expenses, interview expenses, book transport and petty cash.

The figure for books requires further examination. It should be first realized that this percentage represents a total of various book expenditures, not just a single simple sum spent entirely at the discretion of the university librarian. The commonest system in university libraries is to divide the amount available under various headings, principally: 'departmental allocations', general reserve, 'special purchases', 'reading-room' or 'multiple' copies.

It has been traditional in British university libraries to divide up most of what was never a very large cake into allocations to each of the university's academic departments. This was done to ensure an equitable division of resources, or at least to give the appearance of equity. Such advantages as there are to the system are summarized by Donald Davinson in *Academic and legal deposit libraries* as follows: one, the allocations lead to a closer contact between the librarian and the departments and ensure the best use of specialist advice; two, they act as a control on 'unusually voracious departments'; and three,

19

the division of funds by department helps the librarian to see what the pressing needs are and so enables him to justify his estimates.

Woledge and Page, on the other hand, quite properly stress the disadvantages of the system. The first and most obvious point is to query whether it is possible in fact to determine an allocation fairly: should it for instance be based on the current number of staff, students, and research students, or on the amount previously spent? Two other factors which come into consideration are first, do the books in the subject cost more than in others (for example, books on law and medicine are very expensive); and two, how strong is the library's collection in the subject already? The truth is that any allocation by department is almost certain to be arbitrary. A second major disadvantage, pointed out both in Davinson and in Woledge and Page, is the problem of under-spending and over-spending: a progressive department can have its wings unnecessarily and insensitively clipped by the system, while at the other extreme, a department can spend its allocation non-purposively just to ' get its share '. A third major argument against the system is the risk the library runs of having an unbalanced stock: if a department uses its allocation to purchase highly-specialized materials, the general stock in that subject can be neglected entirely; thus the incumbent of a chair can spend a decade or two pursuing a narrow area of interest, so that his successor, as far as the library is concerned, has to start all over again. The fourth and worst feature is, as Woledge and Page note, that ' any such departmentalization of funds is apt to mean a departmentalization of the library itself ': a professor is apt to refer to ' his ' books in the library.

All in all, there is very little to be said in favour of rigidly-applied departmental allocations. However, the system is traditional, and what libraries have had to do has been somehow to liberalize it and make it more flexible. One way has been to promote a less possessive interpretation of the word ' allocation '. Reading University Library, for example, uses instead the term ' target figure ': that is, doing no more than offer the idea that there is a suggested figure of expenditure at which a department should aim. However, the standard and most effective device is to retain a good proportion of the book budget as a general reserve fund, thereby leaving uncommitted money in the librarian's control. This he can use for many purposes: the purchase of an unexpectedly-offered collection, for example; the building-up and maintenance of reference books, printed catalogues, and bibliographies; and exceptional help in a particular subject area. There is also the need to make non-recurrent grants to various departments: that is, to specify a sum over and above the standard annual allocation for the use of a particular department—usually when a new subject area is initiated, or to launch a new professor. A further need is the provision of multiple copies of student textbooks: in any university a large number of students tend to be required to read a relatively small number of standard titles, and thus the provision of only a single copy of such a title is entirely inadequate. One system is to provide one copy of a much-used book in the ordinary loan collection, and to deposit a second copy, for reference only and not for loan (except perhaps over-night or at weekends), in an undergraduate collection. The other common system is to buy multiple copies and to make some of these for consultation only within the library. It is difficult to estimate just how much of the library's book fund should be devoted to this need. There is the point, often stressed, that students are under some obligation to buy standard books for themselves. In some universities secondary collections of such books are available elsewhere in the university—for example, in the library of a hall of residence. However, it is fair to say that the provision of an undergraduate collection is relatively inexpensive. At Reading University, with a student population of 5,000, there is an undergraduate collection which, though perfectly adequate, still does not number above 7,000 titles, and is successfully maintained for about £5,000 annually.

The remaining element in this analysis of a university library budget, periodicals, requires further examination also. To begin with, the sum for periodicals is not normally departmentalized, but is administered as one general fund. The problems attached to operating a periodicals fund, however, are now very considerable indeed. The main problem is that of inflation. In a letter to the *Library Association record* (January 1972), G D E Soar and J W Scott pointed out that if a library paid £6,000 for 1,000 current periodicals in 1964/5, it would need about £12,000 in 1971 just to keep the same 1,000 titles going. This has meant that in recent years most British university libraries have been obliged to curtail subscriptions to new periodicals; but even so, the effect has been that while librarians have also been buying fewer books because of inflation, they have nevertheless by and large been maintaining periodical subscriptions, with the result that the percentage of their budget going on periodicals has begun to overtake that spent on books. In their letter, Soar and Scott refuse to regard this as an unimportant shift of equilibrium between bibliographical forms, but point out that: ' Books are, broadly speaking, more characteristically used by arts than by science students, and by under- than post-graduates, and conversely with periodicals. So that to have a very marked bias towards periodicals-spending is to cater more for the sciences and for research students '.

The preceding paragraphs have been concerned with a simple analysis of a university library's book fund. This is one of a number of exercises which a university librarian has to perform in the preparation of both his annual estimates and his quinquennial estimates. These estimates fall into a number of principal categories: staff, library vote, special services, equipment.

Staff estimates are relatively straightforward. Most librarians inherit a staff establishment, rather than create one. Hence it is usually simple to establish where the current pressures in the various library departments are, and to consult with the heads of such departments as to extra staff required. There are many pointers: for example, if a university's student population suddenly increases in number, it is reasonable to expect that more assistants will be needed in the library's service areas; or if a larger bookfund has been made available to the library, extra staff will be needed to process the increased number of items purchased. The other type of staff need is when the library sets up a new service or a new venture: an extensive reclassification programme, for example, will need appropriate staffing. In such new departures, of course, the librarian has to perform some very careful calculations of staff-time needed, and to decide which grades of staff are required for the operations being contemplated. In quinquennial estimating, he has to look well ahead and try to plot the growth of the library in relation to the growth and development of the university: and then translate what he foresees into terms of staff establishment.

The library vote covers all the headings in the Dammers analysis.

Here it is not just a matter (hard enough as that is) of forecasting what is required in the way of books, periodicals, binding and sundries, but also of forecasting with reasonable accuracy what will be the inevitable annual rise in prices.

Special services cover areas such as photographic and bindery operations. A library photographic department is subject to much the same pressures as the library itself: pressure of work, requiring additional staff; increases in materials costs, requiring additional finance.

Estimates are also required for equipment: shelving, tables and chairs, office furniture and the like. Again the librarian has to establish where and what the need is, and also what that need is likely to become.

Finally, since library estimates are very rarely fully met, the librarian is obliged to add some notes on his priorities: to pick out what he *must* have under each heading.

Estimates are a matter of examining the current and prospective local situation intently. The librarian can employ all sorts of arguments in support of his case; he can refer to rises in the number of students and academic staff; he can link his estimates to what he would take to be an appropriate percentage of the university's total expenditure; he can point to special developments in teaching and research interests at the university. He can also make comparison between his library and other libraries, if it suits his case. There is no standard rule as to the arguments he should use; all are suspect one way or another, but all tend nevertheless to have some degree of relevance.

A development of recent years, especially in America, has been ' performance ' budgeting and ' programme ' budgeting. This begins with a statement of objectives: for example, to catalogue 10,000 titles of a backlog each year for three years; or to set up a branch library. Then comes ' programming '—which, in the words of Rogers and Weber, is to ' state in detail the cost of attaining the objective, drawing on experience '. As Rogers and Weber further note, a set of estimates built along these lines ' permits the budgeting authority to make decisions in terms of objectives with accompanying price tags (sometimes called " cost benefit analysis ")'. A specific application of this method is illustrated in Raffel and Shishko's cost-benefit study of the MIT libraries, *Systematic analysis of university libraries*; and J E

Keller, in his article *Program budgeting and cost benefit analysis in libraries*, follows the idea through to its logical conclusion, and suggests a provocative, if unlikely, solution to the financial problems of university libraries: 'A student fee could be applied to an internal pricing schedule in a library. Students could actually be charged in cash or at the end of a term for the library services they drew upon, or all registered students could get an automatic library allowance that would be drawn upon every time they use the library. Once given its building, grounds, collections, and equipment, a library under this arrangement would turn into a so-called working capital fund which would support itself through the sale of its services. This would furnish to the library a dedicated fund source that would make it financially independent.'

When the librarian has had his estimates considered by his library committee; when these estimates have been forwarded to the vice-chancellor for consideration by various appropriate university planning and finance committees; and when finally he receives notification of what in the end has been granted to him, he then has to make his budget. Theoretically, if his estimates were fully answered, they would logically constitute his budget; but since, as has been remarked already, this rarely happens, what the librarian then has to do is to cut a lesser coat from a reduced amount of cloth: and again he needs to seek the approval of his library committee. During the course of the ensuing year, he has to try to keep within this budget, especially in regard to his library vote. The university's administration department will keep him within his staff establishment; the library vote, however, being divided among books, periodicals, binding and sundries, needs to be continuously accounted for—not just what has been spent, but also what has been committed. His financial records should not be over-elaborate, but they must be sufficient to satisfy his university's accounts department.

Finally, if it has been acknowledged that the library is the university's central organ, it follows that that organ must be properly supported financially. It should not be subject, as it so frequently is, to what Paul Buck in *Libraries and universities* calls the ' crippling alternations of feast and famine '. Steady financial support is essential to good planning. It is important that the librarian should establish credibility within his institution. On this subject Rogers and Weber have some twenty-four carat observations: ' In summary, the budgetary process relies to an extraordinary extent on objective information and well-defined and accepted goals. The library director who has developed his goals on a broad base that includes general university administrative agreement, who has taken the trouble to isolate ratios that are widely accepted or that can be honestly demonstrated on analogy with other libraries, whose budget requests are not capricious but will stand close scrutiny, and who operates in his fiscal management as well as in his requests on the principle of openness and integrity is likely to get an even break for the library. In the last analysis, the library should be of a size and nature appropriate to the rest of the university, and the director should emphasize that he is not building his own empire but is strengthening the entire university '.

II

THE ROLE OF THE UNIVERSITY LIBRARIAN

QUALIFICATIONS: In *The university library in violent transition* (one of the series of University of Tennessee Library Lectures, published in collected form as *The library in the university*), Ralph E Ellsworth complains with some justification that ' we don't know what a librarian is, what he's supposed to do, or how to educate him.' What we do know though, again in Ellsworth's words, is what the university librarian is expected to be: ' a fund-raiser, a campus politician, a learned man and a reader of books, an expert on electronics, and an expert in the science of management '—not to mention ' the small problem of keeping out of jail because the technology of photo-reproduction has gotten far ahead of the copyright laws '. One can sympathize with Ellsworth's temptation at library conventions to ' hole up in a hotel room with our own kind and play poker ', but nevertheless the investigation of the identity and role of a university librarian must be pursued.

However, there is not even a clear pattern as to what formal qualifications are to be expected of a university librarian. To say, as a minimum, that he must be a graduate cannot be taken as a universal truth, because there are exceptions even to this. It is, though, the basic standard qualification. From this common factor, there are two lines of development: one towards scholarship (represented in the form of a higher degree), and the other towards professional attainment (represented in the form of a qualification in librarianship). The ideal is held to be a combination of these: but those so qualified are rare birds indeed. Less rare, but still in the minority, are librarians with higher degrees only. The usual combination and probably an adequate one, is a first degree plus a library qualification. What is also usual is that the first degree is a very good one.

There is similarly little pattern in the matter of training. A growing number of British university librarians are library school-trained, and inevitably and fortunately this will be the future pattern. However, with a good number of others, their professional qualification is that of long service and experience. What it is exactly that makes a competent librarian is still not sufficiently understood by anybody: it is not always some combination of formal training and formal qualification. Panizzi, after all, did impressively well without either. Since we must always legislate for the majority, though, it would be fair to conclude that acceptable qualification for a university librarian is a degree and library school training which has led to a librarianship qualification.

It would be wrong, however, to take it that the librarian's education, both professional and educational, should end there. As Ellsworth says, he is expected to know something of management and many other relevant fields. Thus it is almost obligatory for a university librarian to gather, by way of professional courses and conferences, the essentials of management, of personnel work, and of computer applications in so far as they have relevance to his duties. Likewise he cannot divorce himself completely from academic study and research: this can range from learning Russian to editing an Arden Shakespeare. He cannot give up reading either: he is expected to have some special field of knowledge, in addition to respectably wide cultural interests.

Any assessment of the personal qualities needed by a university librarian is on even more uncertain ground. The nearest to a general truth was that expressed by Sir Frank Francis (at the Cornell Library Conference): that the two essential beliefs of a librarian are a belief in the importance and effectiveness of the written word, and a belief in service to people. Another general truth is the librarian's need of the quite standard personal virtues: tact, for example. S J Patmore, in his paper *The qualities required for good management* (published by the South East Division of the Association of Assistant Librarians in a collection called *Management for librarians*), provides an awesome list of ' executive virtues ':

' 1 The ability wisely to delegate authority.
2 The ability to estimate accurately another's capacity.
3 Power to keep a group working to a common goal.
4 A voice that suggests confidence.
5 A liking for making decisions.
6 An ability to give clear-cut instructions.
7 A habit of seeking new and improved methods.

8 Freedom from prejudice.

9 A calm acceptance of criticism.

10 A willingness to receive suggestions from subordinates.

11 An ability to praise work without fulsome flattery.

12 An ability to criticise work constructively, without antagonising.

13 The habit of giving reasons for orders and seeing that they are understood.

14 Courage to take responsibility for one's own blunders and those of one's subordinates.

15 The habit of using facts and not " hunches ".

16 Quickness in reaching decisions without " going off half-cock ".

17 A sense of humour.

18 An ability to see a vision of achievement.

19 The faculty of seeing the objective steadily and seeing it whole.'

It would be fair to comment that the possession of even a reasonable proportion of these would be sufficient in most cases. Anybody possessing all nineteen would surely be better employed in work of major national priority. However, this exhaustive list does indicate the wide range of personal qualities a librarian requires: every one of them, taken singly, can be justified. Patmore also sees the need to develop a confident manner, to possess considerable intelligence, and to be adaptable to change; and two prominent characteristics are: ' loyalty to the organization of which one is part ', and ' the possession and development of powers of leadership '.

UNIVERSITY ROLE

The librarian is a chief officer of his university, and is invariably listed as such, along with the vice-chancellor, the registrar and the bursar. He is also of professorial status, and except in a very few universities, a member of senate. It is this very dichotomy which is the root of his difficulty in establishing his university identity and role. On the one hand, as a chief officer, he is executive and administrative; on the other, being professorial, his true identification is with teaching and research.

He attends senate *ex officio*. His actual contributions to its deliberations tend to be limited to library matters or to matters which have explicit implications for the library. He can only participate partially in what takes up the greater part of senate's time: discussions and decisions relating to the conduct and organization of the university's teaching and research activities. The major value of membership of the senate for the librarian is that it keeps him in complete touch with all academic developments, because it is in the light of such developments that he must necessarily plan and operate the university's library facilities and services.

He has a similar role and derives a similar benefit from membership of other academic bodies within the university: Faculty Boards, for example. He must represent and speak for the library, and he must take cognizance of all that has relevance in library terms. An obvious example of the latter would be any proposal to launch a new and major field of study: setting up a Department of Law, say, or a School of Architecture. In library terms, ventures such as these would require an outlay of several tens of thousands of pounds on appropriate books and journals.

It would be wrong to assume that the librarian has no right to any other role in the university than that connected with his professional capacity. Plainly, the librarian in his own right as an individual might be very interested in sports activities, or German studies, or military training: and therefore earn a quite personal place on relevant university bodies. But by and large his usual role on university bodies is as an *ex officio* member; and in many areas of such membership, this role is necessarily the passive one of an observer.

The first point in Paul Buck's ' Library administrator's credo ' is that a librarian in a university is above all an interpreter, an interpreter of ' his profession and his institution . . . to those who use the library '. He is the link, as Woledge and Page note, between the library and the teaching staff. That is why most librarians are ardent senior common room men. It is over coffee and lunch and tea that they conduct much of their business with their academic colleagues.

However, unlike their academic colleagues, they are charged with a very great administrative responsibility: a large building, a considerable number of staff, a sizeable budget, a complicated system of technical and professional routines—and the whole university to serve. It is these administrative duties which occupy most of the librarian's time.

Fortunately, as Nigel Cox comments in *Management criteria in the design of systems for academic libraries,* 'the attitude that the librarian need only be a scholar and that any fool could manage a library' must now be dead. There seems to be a general realization that the management of a library is an arduous and skilful business. Just how arduous and skilful becomes readily apparent when the librarian's administrative duties are itemized and described.

The librarian's duties in relation to his library committee have already been described. So too have those concerned with estimating and budgeting. Connected with estimating are the first two duties of any administrator: to forecast and to plan. It is the librarian alone who can plot the optimum development of the library, because no one else, neither on his own staff nor in the university generally, can possess all the available pieces of relevant information and interpret this information in library terms. The librarian knows the capacity of his present library service, and can match against this demands likely to be made on it by the further growth of the university—in terms of accommodation, of finance, and of staff. Such forecasting and planning obliges the librarian to produce an almost continuous stream of reports and memoranda, usually solicited but sometimes not. A set of estimates can take days to prepare; a development plan weeks to prepare; a building plan years to prepare.

Forecasting and planning are to do with the future. In the day-to-day present, the librarian has to organize. Gelfand provides a concise summary of what such organizing entails: '(a) identifying the particular activities which are or should be carried out, and grouping them by broad function; (b) arranging the functions in homogeneous units, or departments, if the size of the staff warrants; (c) defining precisely the responsibilities and duties of each unit; and (d) defining the lines of authority and the relationships that should exist within and among the units or departments.' The result of (a) is that the librarian is able to see his library in its essential aspects: its administrative element, its reader services, its technical processes. The result of (b) is a further necessary refinement: to see technical processes, for example, in terms of an acquisitions department, a cataloguing department, a preparations department, a bindery. The result of (c) is to see each of those further components in terms of what they should be doing and how they should be doing it. The result of (d) is establishing a chain of command, a flow of work, and a co-ordinating network: for example, that there should be a sub-librarian in charge of the acquisitions department; that that sub-librarian should be directly responsible to the deputy librarian; that the work of the acquisitions department must necessarily dovetail with that of the cataloguing department.

To achieve what is entailed by (b), (c) and (d) requires what Henri Fayol, one of the pioneers of administrative theory, called ' command ': staffing, making decisions, and providing the right atmosphere. It means, in fact, driving the machine so created. Fayol also indicated the obvious corollary to this: the need for control—to check the outcome of all of this organization, to measure the results against the plan. It takes nervous energy to drive the machine; it takes eternal vigilance to see that it is not failing in any area. The librarian cannot, and should not, try to do all the driving and all the checking himself: he must be able to delegate a great deal. This after all is the reason for his setting up an administrative hierarchy.

Three specific areas of a librarian's administrative duties deserve further emphasis. These are staffing, the provision and maintenance of accommodation and equipment, and building up the library's stock.

Staffing (a further treatment of this whole topic follows in Chapter III) is obviously a key element in the organizational and administrative plan. The librarian has to establish what staff are required for the service he proposes, in precise terms of grade and number; he has to attract, choose, and appoint such staff; to see that they are trained; and to see that they are adequately supervised. Being in charge of staff brings in its train a great deal of personnel work: not only such practical matters as salary scales, promotions, and transfers, but also the more human side in which the librarian as the head of the team becomes a combination of confessor, arbitrator, counsellor and even psychiatrist. In this second area the librarian has to tread warily, but it is nevertheless a valid call on his time. If libraries could be staffed with automatons they would be very easy institutions to run; if decisions and changes could be made without having to worry about the reactions of the staff concerned, no doubt an efficient and logical organization would be more readily achieved. However since staff are not automatons and do react, the importance of this side of the librarian's personnel work must be ranked very high. It might be added that it is also one of the greatest time-consumers.

The provision and maintenance of accommodation and equipment also arises naturally, like staffing, from Gelfand's summary of the librarian's organizational responsibility. Just as he has to plan in staff terms, he has also to plan how they and their functions are to be housed and equipped. Even when no new major accommodation or equipping is called for, there is the constant month-to-month need for adjustment and replacement. The librarian has the overall responsibility to maintain the fabric of his building, even though he may delegate this to somebody else on his staff. There is a perpetual involvement with the janitors and the cleaners; and the builders, electricians, carpenters, painters and engineers. The librarian's responsibility for control extends, in the final analysis, even to the rapid replacement of an electric light bulb in the bookstack.

Building up the bookstock does not fit neatly into the librarian's administrative structure. True enough, he will have set up an acquisitions department, properly staffed and with an approved set of clerical routines; he will also have established the regular channels through which book and journal recommendations should come. But it does not really end there. In this area the librarian is not just an administrator: he is the editor and creator of an active and essential stock, and this is drawing on his personal, professional and bibliographical attainments rather than on his managerial abilities. This is where librarianship is as much an art as it is a science.

A point arises from the above which deserves to be made before concluding any description of a librarian's administrative duties. It is that, true enough, the organization and management of a library cannot be regarded as an occupation for untrained scholars; but neither can it solely be regarded in bureaucratic or office terms. A university library is not a government department, or an insurance office, or a department store. A librarian is obliged to ask the right managerial questions—what, why, when, where, how, who?—but he must remember in answering these questions that his true brief is to remain an educator and a librarian. As the Booz, Allen and Hamilton report on

Problems in university library management commented: ' Improved management methods alone will not guarantee good libraries, sensitive to and capable of meeting the needs of their users. Research libraries are educational in their essence, and effective management is only one of a number of elements required to meet their service obligations '.

PROFESSIONAL ACTIVITIES

As well as having a university role and an administrative role, the librarian is also an important representative of his profession.

He sees this most frequently in his dealings with his own staff. To them he is the ultimate guide on all professional matters. He is usually automatically eligible to be considered so by virtue of possessing longer and wider experience than theirs.

He invariably acts as a career adviser, not just to his own staff, but also to would-be entrants to librarianship as a profession. His work in the latter area is often done in conjunction with the university's appointments officer. Students interested in taking up librarianship as a career come to him, singly and in groups, for his advice. Part of such work has an element of self-interest: often what begins as a request for advice becomes an interview for a post and therefore a means of recruitment. The librarian can extend such activity outside his university: to local schools, for example. His professional advice is also sought by a wide range of people on all matters to do with books and publication: how to compile a bibliography, how to prepare a work for publication, which bookseller to approach in connection with the sale of a back-run of a journal.

Within the ranks of his own profession, he also has a role to fill and responsibilities to undertake. On a national level, he may be involved in the work of the Library Association as an officer or council member; he may serve on one or more of its committees; he may be active in one of its sections; he may share in the conduct of its examinations. He will be a member of the Standing Conference of National and University Libraries, attending its conferences, and perhaps be a member of its main committee or one or more of its sub-committees. He might even have a place on an international body: the International Federation of Library Associations, for example. He will also have a local role: either in connection with the local branch of the Library Association, or in some other local grouping of library interests. The librarian can also serve on national non-library bodies: government committees, the Association of University Teachers, or one of the specialist committees of the British Standards Institution. He might also serve on the governing body of one of the national libraries. Yet again, there are national committees where the common factor is a special subject (for example, Latin American library materials) or a particular technical area of librarianship (for example, microforms or computer applications).

Professionally, too, he must interest himself in and work for all relevant co-operative ventures, whether international or national or regional. Examples of such ventures are more fully treated in chapter VIII. A librarian needs to participate in the improvement and exploitation of the whole network of library resources.

In his own right he may wish to contribute to the literature of his profession, usually in the form of articles for library and educational journals, sometimes in the form of books. He most frequently does this by developing a knowledge of one or more special aspects of his profession—library buildings, say, or mechanization. In the same way and on the same grounds, he may give lectures and addresses.

On the basis of the foregoing sections, it will be seen that there is some justification for Ellsworth's dispirited remarks. A university librarian is a fully-, even over-stretched individual, trying hard to combine his personal, university, administrative and professional roles. He has a multiple identity and multiple responsibilities, and his brief seems occasionally to be the impossible one of being all things to all men.

III

UNIVERSITY LIBRARY STAFF

GRADES: The Association of University Teachers in its pamphlet *The university library* commented: ' It cannot be too strongly emphasised that the quality of the library service ultimately depends upon the quality of the people entering it '. In line with this view was the joint statement of the AUT and the Library Association in 1963 recommending that there should be straight equivalence in grades and salaries between graduate library staff and teaching staff.

The obvious point to make here is that the key staff of a university library are graduates. Non-graduates are employed, but it cannot be said that there is any really satisfactory career scale for them.

A graduate entrant to university librarianship begins as an assistant librarian. Normal qualifications for appointment to this grade are a good honours degree, and a qualification in librarianship or a research degree. A qualification in librarianship is more usual than a research degree, and possession of both is very unusual indeed, despite the persistently maintained view that such a combination would be highly desirable. The assistant librarianship is the career grade, and the salary scale should be the university lecturer's scale. In most libraries the last part of the scale usually carries with it the title of sub-librarian, and progress to a sub-librarianship is not automatic, but depends on promotion and the assumption of additional responsibilities: usually the headship of a division of the library's work.

The next salary scale in a university is that for readers and senior lecturers. In the majority of libraries this scale is reserved for the deputy librarian, though it can also be used, wholly or partially, for senior sub-librarians.

The final university scale is the professorial scale, which should apply to the university librarian. The AUT/Library Association statement recommended this most strongly; it further recommended that there should be no distinction in salary scale between the librarian of a large university and the librarian of a small university, making the

35

point that the 'small library, particularly the library which has to be built up from scratch in a new university institution, has specially difficult and pressing problems of development, and it is essential that in such institutions the librarian should be gifted in energy, intellect, imagination and experience, if the development is to be satisfactory'. The statement adds that if some distinction is felt to be necessary between the various sizes of institution, this can be made within the range of the professorial scale. It is worth noting here that university librarians, like professors, are appointed to a point on the professorial scale, and there is no subsequent automatic incremental progress.

It must be remarked in conclusion that there is as yet no standard national pattern of grades and salaries for university library staff, despite the efforts of the AUT and the Library Association. There are libraries which have in fact achieved for their staff the recommended equivalence with academic staff; but there are others which still pay their staffs as if they were low-grade clerical assistants. Most libraries have, however, achieved the kind of arrangements described. Indeed, as M B Line notes in his article *Staffing university libraries,* 'the entrant with qualifications comparable to those of a university teacher, especially if he has a higher degree, can probably expect to achieve promotion more rapidly than most university teachers'.

The AUT and the Library Association have recently agreed a new joint statement which gives guidelines for further negotiations based on the principles outlined in the 1963 document. Three grades of graduate library staff are proposed. Librarian Grade III would be the career grade of university graduate librarians, the salary scale running from the bottom of the lecturer's scale to the top, and subject to the same efficiency bar at the appropriate point on the lecturer's scale. Librarian Grade II would be a selective grade for posts carrying a higher level of administrative and professional responsibility, or requiring specialist knowledge; the salary scale would run from the bottom to the top of the senior lecturer's scale. Librarian Grade I would be the grade for the member of staff designated deputy librarian, the salary starting at the professorial minimum. As in the original joint statement, the chief librarian would have professorial status and emoluments.

36

As was mentioned earlier, university libraries also employ non-graduate staff. Numerically, the largest group here are the library assistants, or juniors. These are boys and girls with o levels and a couple of A levels. They are not regarded as being very permanent: 'wastage' is high. Marriage or some form of higher education claim most of them eventually. Those who wish to stay in librarianship tend to go on to the two year full time course at library school; afterwards, they can pursue their career more successfully in a county, public or special library. Most libraries have a grade above library assistant—sometimes called senior library assistant—where the equivalence is with the AP scales: but for an ambitious person this is not usually sufficient. The same grade is often used for graduates without professional qualification, though the AUT/Library Association statement did recommend for such entrants the application of a probationary period of not more than five years.

In addition to library assistants, a university library will also employ various secretarial assistants. The salaries for both these categories vary regionally, but are often linked with local government scales. There will also be technical staff—photographers and binders, for example—who will be paid according to either university technician scales or at appropriate trade union rates. Finally, there will be janitorial and perhaps cleaning staff, who again will be paid appropriate standard rates.

STRUCTURE

Until very recently, the standard staff structure in a British university library has been a pyramidal one. At the top is the university librarian —forecasting and planning, organizing, commanding, co-ordinating, controlling. Below him is the deputy librarian, responsible for the day-to-day operation of the library. Below these again, are the heads of the major sections of the library—acquisitions (or order) department, cataloguing department, reader services. Within each of these three major sections, there will be a further hierarchy: a second-in-command, staff with special areas of responsibility, junior staff for routine and clerical operations. What led to this pattern, as Kenneth Humphreys explains in his article *The subject specialist in national and university libraries*, was the weight given to the processing functions in libraries. It should be added that this development was a perfectly sound one: a necessary rationalization as library operations grew in volume and in complexity. What also resulted, unfortunately, was a tendency to rigid and inflexible compartmentalization of library staffs. Even now it is difficult in some libraries to persuade a member of staff that he is a member of a whole library team rather than exclusively a cataloguer or an orderer of books. A side-effect of this is the not infrequent inter-sectional rivalries and discords: the general reputation of the library tends to be put second to the concerns of particular sections of it, and the purpose and justification of the entire enterprise lost sight of all too frequently. Moreover, as Robert P Haro has pointed out in his article on *Change in academic libraries*, functional specialization heads the list of those ' bureaucratic phenomena ' which are barriers to change and innovation in a library.

Administratively the system described above works very well, and the routine processing duties are performed efficiently and expertly. However, it will be obvious that the users of the library gain very little benefit from whatever subject skills or knowledge the library staff have—for example, a cataloguer with a considerable personal knowledge of the social sciences might be able to bring such knowledge to bear on classifying books in that field, but his opportunities to give reference and bibliographical help to readers will probably be confined to the one night each week during term when he is on late duty at the library's enquiry desk. From his own point of view too, such a prospect can be unattractive: he is after all deriving very little benefit from, and adding very little to, his basic academic interests. To waste a first class honours degree in French, say, on book ordering routines, is waste indeed.

There has now begun, consequently, a movement towards the organization of university libraries by subject rather than by function (see Chapter VI). The structure then tends to be less hierarchical, more of a necklace than a pyramid—a string of subject specialists with the librarian as the central stone. This image is not altogether frivolous, because one of the drawbacks of the subject specialist structure is, as Davinson points out, that specialists ' run the risk of being kept aside from the main promotion stream through lack of opportunity to prove general administrative ability '. The university librarian's solitary splendour is altogether too solitary. The advantage of the division by function was that an assistant librarian could readily observe the rungs of the career ladder. Within a library department, his first step was by application and intelligence to demonstrate his competence in the functions of that department. In not too long a while, this competence would be acknowledged by promotion to a higher level in the department—to second-in-command and eventually, either in his own library or in a similar one elsewhere, to departmental headship. This position then allowed him to gain administrative experience, in managing a set of routines, in superintending a team and in producing results both in quantity and in quality. On the basis of such administrative experience, he would eventually be able to apply for a post as deputy librarian, which in turn was the stepping-stone (in, on average, a period as short as two years) to a university librarianship. The route for a subject specialist is by no means so clear-cut. The tendency seems to be to equate subject specialization with the official career grade of the lecturer's scale. This is fine from the point of view of the university librarian, who after all has no further worries concerning his own career; but it must cause a little concern to the subject specialist himself.

It is worthwhile at this point to define the term ' subject specialist ' a little more precisely. Humphreys supplies such a definition: ' a subject specialist is a member of a library staff appointed to develop one or more aspects of a library's technical or reference service in a particular subject field. Although he would normally already have some experience in this field and would commonly have obtained a first or research degree in the subject it is not essential that he should have qualifications in the subject when he is appointed '.

Both Line and Humphreys stress what is an important outcome of the subject specialist system. This is that it will surely aid libraries in their attempts to recruit staff of a high quality. Plainly, a graduate with a good honours degree is bound to be deterred by the prospect of devoting his life to some routine library operation. However, if he is able to work usefully in a library and at the same time maintain his academic connection with, and academic status in, a subject, then he is much more likely to be attracted to librarianship as a profession.

A university library is a service institution, and the quality of its service depends primarily on the quality of its staff. Thus if a university librarian can attract, select and retain good staff, he has gone most of the way towards achieving an effective library service. Good staff selection may seem something of an intuitive art, but the basic elements can be reduced to a number of entirely practical devices and principles. A very helpful book on the subject is Elizabeth Sidney and Margaret Brown's *The skills of interviewing*.

The very first step before inviting applications is, obviously, to establish what the post to be advertised is, what duties are to be performed, and what sort of person would best fill it. Staff selection ranges from, say, the appointment of a library assistant for the enquiry desk, to the appointment of a deputy librarian. The former kind of appointment tends to be made by the university librarian (probably with the advice and assistance of the head of the library department concerned), the latter by a sub-committee of the library committee, with the university librarian in attendance. Defining the need for the post and describing its functions are relatively simple matters in the case of an established post falling vacant; the more difficult operation is when a new post is being created. Filling a vacancy is to a large extent a formality; creating a post needs to be debated with the senior staff of the library, and negotiated with the library committee and the university. The most usual reasons for creating a post are either pressure of work on existing staff, or the setting-up of an entirely new venture.

The next stage is to consider the kind of applicant required. The person required for the post of library assistant at the enquiry desk, for example, would probably be a boy or girl of eighteen or nineteen, with some o levels and perhaps two A levels, and preferably with an interest in librarianship as a career; additionally, there might be the need for the possession of some special skill such as typing. The person required for the post of deputy librarian would need to be highly qualified academically and professionally, and possess a considerable amount of senior library experience; additionally, the library concerned might require an interest or specialization in a particular subject field—computerization, for example, or the social sciences.

For both posts, specific personal qualities will be looked for—such as (for the library assistant) a pleasant, outgoing manner, a methodical mind, an interest in books, and an interest in people; and for the deputy librarian, an ability to get things done, a gift for organization, a way with people, loyalty and enthusiasm.

A suitable advertisement can now be drafted: naming and briefly describing the post, stating the qualifications sought, indicating the salary offered, and giving the name of the university officer (usually the librarian or the registrar) to whom applications should be sent and by which date. Advertisements for posts above the level of library assistant invariably ask candidates to give the names of referees who can be approached to supply an opinion as to their merits. In addition to an advertisement, it is usual to prepare for senior posts a sheet of ' further particulars ', in which a much fuller account is given of the job, the library, and the various conditions of service offered by the university. In the advertisement itself it should be mentioned that such ' further particulars ' are available to would-be applicants on request. Junior posts such as those as library assistant are ordinarily advertised only in the local newspaper; more senior posts are advertised in national newspapers such as the *Times*, the *Guardian* and the *Telegraph*, and in the *Library Association record*, but most commonly in what is in effect the librarian's trade paper, the *Times literary supplement*.

The next step is for the librarian, assisted probably by his deputy librarian or another member of his senior staff, to study the applications immediately after the advertised closing date, and to make a short list from them of candidates who seem worthy of interview. Again it is worth making the distinction between the approach required for a junior post and that required for more senior posts. Applications for library assistant posts tend to be in the form of a short, simple letter, stating the post sought, the age of the candidate, the school he or she attends or attended, and his or her educational attainments. Something can be deduced from the school named: often a library has been particularly fortunate, or unfortunate, in its experience with pupils from a given school. Even more, indeed most, can be deduced from the applicant's educational attainments—good A levels, for example, are not easily come by; and a fair range of O levels, preferably including a foreign language or languages, is another good guide. The other factor is the overall impression made by the letter; is it clear and unstilted in its style, is it neat and meticulous in appearance? Library assistants cannot be chosen solely on the basis of a letter, since the need for a good personality is obviously such a key issue: but letters can tell a great deal, and they certainly are the basis on which interviews are invited.

An application for a senior post is a very much more formal affair. It can be made in the form of a letter which is supported by a full *curriculum vitae,* or on an officially-supplied application form, or presented in tabulated form by the applicant himself. No matter what manner of presentation is used, the same basic information is offered: the name of the post applied for; the applicant's name and address; his present position; the salary he is currently earning; his date of birth and marital status; schools and university attended; academic and professional qualifications; languages known; other relevant activities and attainments; a complete statement of professional experience; a description of present duties; a list of publications; and finally, the names and addresses of his referees. Presentation is plainly not the main issue here (though of course it is never unimportant): what is looked for is the quality of the first degree, professional qualifications, and the relevance of the professional experience gained so far. Once a short list has been decided on, the next step is to write to the candidates' referees, at the same time inviting the short-listed candidates for interview.

Interviews for both junior and senior staff must be carefully planned. Sidney and Brown summarize the purpose of interviews thus: ' In broad terms, they must determine the candidate's suitability, create goodwill for the company, and explain the job '. The first of these three aims will be examined in more detail in subsequent paragraphs. The second aim, that of creating goodwill for the library, is important in that the impression made on all candidates, whether they are successful or not, must be an excellent one if the library hopes to continue to attract good staff; and it is achieved by courtesy, hospitality, charm and unequivocal fairness. The last aim is also important; an interview is a two-way operation: the candidate himself must be quite certain as to what is being offered and what would be required of him.

To aim to determine a candidate's suitability for an important post in a matter of thirty to forty five minutes obviously entails the detailed planning of interviews. The preliminary basic routine for interviewing at both junior and senior level is for the university librarian (in the case of junior appointments) or the chairman of the interviewing sub-committee (in the case of senior appointments) to take the candidate step-by-step through his written application. In advance, the librarian and the other interviewers will have noted questions to ask the candidate: usually to elicit information additional to the bare outline of the actual application, often to query gaps or ambiguities in the candidate's *curriculum vitae*. This is the part of the interview for which the candidate should be especially well prepared: this is where he makes his first impression on the librarian and/or committee. By the same token, on the interviewers' side, this is where, bearing in mind the requirements of the post in question, they confirm the candidate's formal claims to consideration for it. Sidney and Brown recount what happened at successfully conducted interviews: 'Although the effective interviewers seldom seemed to impose restrictions on the applicant's responses, they were none the less persistently guided by certain broad objectives that led them to obtain a connected and coherent biography and to dwell on those aspects of his life history likely to prove most informative'. The other major piece of advice given by Sidney and Brown to interviewers is that they must open ' each new topic with a general rather than with a detailed question '. The reasons for such advice can be readily understood. One straightforward one is that to launch abruptly into an unheralded detailed question could unsettle the candidate to no purpose whatsoever; he and the interviewers must be allowed to work into a topic gradually. Another reason is that a general question makes the candidate choose a particular tack—and which tack precisely, can be very revealing in itself; the interviewers are then able to pursue the candidate's line in detail, and how he acquits himself is most revealing of all.

Sidney and Brown itemize usefully the evidence which an interviewer needs to collect. First come a self-explanatory pair: manner and appearance; both are important in library work since in most of its aspects it involves dealing with people; and both are especially important in junior appointments since juniors tend to carry the major burden of everyday dealings with the library's clientele. Next is evidence relating to intelligence: not just ' high intellectual ability ' but also ' commonsense ' and ' understanding '. Intelligence is indicated by educational attainment, by professional achievement, and by private interests *in depth*. Sidney and Brown quote Dr Joseph Hanna (*Educational and psychological assessment,* 1950) on the characteristics of high intelligence, which are: ' outstanding specific aptitudes (*eg* music, mathematics), high scholarship, conversational ability, good habits of application, and good appearance '. The third area of evidence concerns social ability: the ' ability to get on with others, to command or persuade, to initiate or obey '. Fourth is the attitude to authority: evidence that a candidate has learned ' a way of coming to terms with authority which seems to him successful '. Fifth is evidence as to emotional stability and persistence. Sidney and Brown define a stable person as one who: ' does not lose his head in an emergency. He remains able to think clearly and act purposefully in situations that reduce many people to great anxiety. He reaches balanced judgements after reviewing all the evidence. His actions are consistent. What he promises he does.'

Additionally, the interviewers might be looking particularly for administrative ability, and here Sidney and Brown define the qualities involved so that the relevant evidence can be sought: ' an ability to look ahead, to initiate action, to co-ordinate the efforts of other people, to " get things done ", to " organize " '. The relevant evidence here will be the candidate's past performance, as recorded in his *curriculum vitae* and as witnessed by his referees; as Sidney and Brown say, ' past behaviour provides the most reliable evidence on which to predict future behaviour '. Finally, these two authors ask interviewers to explore the candidate's attitude towards himself: ' How does he see himself? What are the sources of his self-respect? '. A blatant example here, known to every librarian who has been involved in interviewing, is the candidate who recounts how he has been dogged by ill-luck and injustice. This might possibly, in very rare cases, be true: but usually it is an excuse for a doubtful career performance. And if it were indeed true, this can hardly count in the candidate's favour, since Napoleon had a perfectly valid point when he required his generals to be, above all else, lucky.

In conclusion, it is worth making a few comments about interviews from the interviewee's point of view. The first thing to remember is that there is nothing unusual or shameful about an unsuccessful interview. For any one vacancy there is normally a short list of four to six candidates, and it is almost entirely a matter of the aforementioned luck as to just how strong the competition is. It could be that particular day, for instance, that one's competitors include God's current gift to librarianship. There is every excuse in that and other cases for failure to obtain the post: often a candidate is an excellent person, but the interviewing committee in his interest choose somebody else. An interview is, as has been remarked, a two-way business: an applicant with certain undeniably good attainments and qualities might just not be particularly appropriate for the post in question. There is, however, very little excuse for not gaining an interview. Something will be found to be wrong here: the post applied for might have been ill-chosen, or the application itself poorly aimed. Sidney and Brown offer a kind of formula for success at interviews: first, try to establish with yourself where your ambitions lie; assess that you possess the necessary brains and ability; gather the necessary training and experience; and present yourself favourably, calmly and civilly—but do not over-relax, because it is after all an interview and not a social engagement. All one can add to this formula is to remind would-be interviewees that there is nothing odd about feeling nervous at the prospect of an interview, nor about reactions such as an initial tendency to halting speech or (equally commonly) an untypical garrulousness. The nervousness and nervous reactions must be controlled and this is best done by remembering that, by and large, interviewing committees are well-disposed and kindly (as they must be, if they wish to find and attract the right candidate) and perfectly capable of making allowance for the candidate's quite natural anxiety. A final thought, though, must be that an interview is no more than a situation to be handled: if one cannot handle it, one cannot claim to be capable of handling whatever other difficult situations there are inherent in the responsibilities of the post itself. It is no use accusing a person of being successful at interviews only because he is confident, quick-thinking, and sensitive to atmospheres: after all, the very same qualities will stand him in equally good stead in the post itself.

45

A library has a duty to further the professional development of its staff members once it has recruited them. In this there are disadvantages for itself, but in a larger way, the whole profession of librarianship is enhanced. The successful training, education and encouragement of a young librarian invariably leads to that young librarian moving on eventually to a higher post elsewhere: but this is exactly how it should be. The library benefits directly from the young librarian's enthusiasm, energy and ideas, for perhaps four or five years; but it draws equal honour from his subsequent career. After all, if a library enjoys the reputation of producing excellent and successful librarians, it will be a magnet for other good candidates. No library flourishes on inbreeding: there must be a constant turnover of personalities, a regular jolting of set ideas and fossilized routines, and repeated injections of new enthusiasms. Not every library takes this view, because of course there are arguments on the other side regarding the undeniable benefits of continuity, long service, loyalty, and background knowledge of that particular library's character, setting and history. But generally speaking, a static staff leads to restricted thinking and restrictive practices.

Gelfand names six main devices to encourage the professional development of a library's staff. The first he calls ' staff orientation ': that is, getting acquainted with the particular library. An obvious instance of this is a preliminary tour of the whole library for each new staff member; this can be done by the librarian himself, or his deputy, or by the head of the section to which the new member has been assigned. This tour should be much more than a ten minute affair, and if it includes visits to various outlying libraries and sections, it should be spread over a period of days or weeks. Its immediate aim should be to introduce the new member personally to the majority of the existing staff. It is similarly helpful if the university librarian arranges to welcome each new member of staff himself on their first day.

Gelfand next mentions a ' staff manual '. This is a detailed written account of every operation which is performed in the library. No library should permit a system where knowledge of the details of the greater part of its operations exists only in various people's heads: life is far too uncertain for this kind of negligence and possessiveness. For a new staff member, a staff manual is essential. If he is taking over an established post, the previous incumbent has usually departed, and all he can learn of the post is what has been written down and what is remembered by others. It is far more effective, and very much less time-consuming, if he can be handed a comprehensive manual which contains a full description of the duties and routines of his particular post. Also, by reading through the entire manual, he learns—equally importantly—the complete context of his own function. Also useful is a staff newsletter or bulletin, issued once a term or more frequently, which communicates to the staff generally information about new developments, services, and procedures. Normally such publications are informal in tone, with contributions from various library departments and individuals, the whole being edited by a senior member of the staff.

Staff meetings are the next device referred to by Gelfand. It is essential to maintain communications in a library: between the university librarian and his senior staff; between the university librarian and his staff generally; among the staff as such; and within individual library departments. In practical terms, this should mean regular and frequent meetings at which the university librarian informs his senior staff (that is, the heads of the various departments of the library) of the issues that are currently concerning the library committee and himself, and at which the senior staff in their turn can air their problems.

It is best to have some kind of agenda for such meetings, even if it is only a list of topics that the librarian has been notified will be raised. It is also important that somebody should be charged with the task of recording the decisions taken at the meeting, both to prevent subsequent misunderstandings, and also to reduce the number of ' chestnuts '—that is, topics which have already received adequate consideration on several previous occasions but which nevertheless tend to re-appear on the agenda. Heads-of-department meetings are likely to be lengthy, since it is difficult and usually unsatisfactory to apply a strict time-limit either to the discussion of individual topics or to the whole session; one useful device, however, it to set up ad hoc groups of staff to wrestle with specific problems which involve much minor detail, rather than have those problems laboured over in full session.

Staff participation in decision-making in a library is important because it is, as Robert P Haro has noted, conducive to innovation and change. Haro further suggests that the ideal arrangement in a library would be to have a permanent planning or research group, to overcome the ' basic resistance to change of a library organization '. Such a research group would ' study, recommend, and seek the implementation of better library service policies and programs ', and would comprise representatives from academic teaching departments, a sample of managerial and non-managerial librarians, and student representatives. To avoid inhibition, the group should not include the librarian, nor the deputy librarian, nor academics of professorial status.

In addition to heads-of-department meetings, there should be departmental meetings, one feature of which should be a report by the department head on matters relevant to the department or its staff which have been discussed at the heads-of-department meeting. Occasionally the university librarian should address his staff as a whole, especially when some major development is in the offing—for example, a new building, or a new way of organizing the library. Among the staff generally, the social contacts of the staff-room and the professional contacts of work can be pursued in a variety of ways out-of-hours: there could be, for example, an occasional seminar on a general professional topic—or a theatre outing. All of such meetings that are relevant help the new member to settle in more successfully; and for the existing staff, they provide a constant stimulus to their professional development.

Gelfand moves next to ' in-service training '. This relates primarily to junior staff, and university libraries have on the whole a very poor record in respect of such training. The usual system has been to assign a junior member of staff to a particular department and leave it at that. The junior becomes proficient in the routines of the department, and unless he or she requests a transfer, or unless a more urgent need arises elsewhere in the library, no subsequent placement is arranged. The only training received is training in the departmental routines with which the junior is to be especially concerned, except perhaps

48

for some connected with relief duties at the library's issue desk. What a junior really needs is an initial series of short-term placements, and to be taught in each the respective routines involved. In addition, there might also be a regular weekly lecture given by each head of department in turn to explain further how the library operates. Short-term placements are best arranged by operating a 'pool' system for new juniors: a junior is not therefore assigned permanently on arrival to a particular department, but regarded for, say, a six-month period, as one of a reserve group making the rounds. The useful and valuable result should be a junior who is an intensively trained all-rounder.

The reasons why such a system is not common in university libraries are unfortunately only too clear. First, university libraries in this country are not generously staffed; there is not sufficient slack to create any sort of 'pool'. Secondly, many university library staffs are in any case far too small to allow such a system. And both these situations produce the state of affairs where a junior vacancy creates such an emergency that the reaction can only be to aim to fill the vacancy as quickly and as permanently as possible. A third reason now is the rapid turnover of junior staff. Most library assistants stay only for one or two years. Quite often a library assistant is somebody filling in a year before going on to university or to some other form of higher education: it is therefore a waste of time to do other than just employ him or her to perform a specific task or tasks.

Two categories of junior staff who must be treated differently, are young graduate staff and library school trainees. The young professionally qualified graduate, or the young graduate who intends to qualify professionally, must be exposed to as many areas of library work as possible. Similarly, the trainee sent by a library school for some weeks of practical experience must be given the opportunity to try his hand at a variety of library routines, to visit most of the library's branches and sections, and to have professional discussions with the senior staff.

The fifth device specified by Gelfand to promote the professional development of staff concerns 'professional activities outside the university'. Staff should be encouraged, and financed, to attend professional meetings and conferences. This is where they will gather new ideas, learn from the experience of senior and nationally-known members of their profession, and make helpful contacts. Similarly, they should be enabled and permitted to attend courses on a wide range of professional topics; and they should be especially helped to attend any course that is particularly relevant to their everyday duties. By the same token, the staff of a university library should be persuaded to visit other libraries: this kind of exposure helps them to assess what they are doing in their own library, to be more critical, and to operate in less of a vacuum.

Finally, Gelfand mentions ' teaching and writing ' on librarianship. It is the patent duty of any library to assist and encourage its staff to make contributions to the expertise and to the literature of librarianship. The university librarian should grant members of his staff the necessary opportunities, facilities and time to pursue such activity. Equally, he should be willing to discuss and debate proposed contributions, and to comment and advise as helpfully as he can. In some cases, he can initiate contributions by deliberately engaging the interest of a suitable member of his staff in a specific topic, and then persuade that member of staff to publish, or lecture on, his findings.

IV

UNIVERSITY LIBRARY STOCK

CATEGORIES OF MATERIAL: What goes to make up the stock of a university library can be analyzed in a variety of ways. The simplest division is in relation to the way in which it automatically reflects the dual role of a university: on the one hand teaching, on the other research. Thus the library provides teaching and learning materials for undergraduates, and research materials for the rest of the university community. Of these two categories of provision the first is by far the easier, because what is required is readily ascertainable and, assuming that there are adequate financial resources, equally readily obtainable. The second category is altogether much more problematical, because there are no precisely-defined upper limits to such provision. J G P Pafford, in his article *Book selection in the university library,* states that research workers need: ' a large library strong in basic general reference works and basic specialized works, including periodicals, in all fields, but also large collections of what is loosely called secondary literature '; and adds that the difficulty lies in the matter of secondary literature, which he reckons to comprise ' perhaps 90 percent of all books '. The Association of University Teachers, in *The university library,* also stressed this need for ' a considerable " peripheral " stock '. It will be appreciated that once one begins to talk of ' secondary ' or ' peripheral ' material as being very necessary, one has abandoned any possibility of setting exact boundaries to a library's stock. An attendant problem is that whereas the purchase of undergraduate material is, relatively speaking, technically straight-forward (since by and large it is in print) and not exceptionally expensive, secondary materials are usually only obtainable secondhand (and therefore make very heavy demands on senior staff time in the matter of searching through booksellers' catalogues, quite apart from the fact that the high prices demanded for such material reflect all too clearly its limited availability).

A slightly fuller analysis of the bookstock of an academic library is presented in Randall and Goodrich's *Principles of college library administration*. Here the authors divide it by function, as follows:

Reference function

Curricula function

General function

Research function.

The second and fourth of these have already been mentioned. An important additional component is the first they mention: the library's provision of books for a variety of reference needs. An academic library is like any other large library in this respect. Not only are bibliographical tools needed—catalogues of major libraries and collections; subject and national bibliographies; list of books in print; union lists of periodicals; abstracts; indexes;—but also all the standard types of reference work—encyclopedias; atlases; gazetteers; biographical dictionaries; language dictionaries; yearbooks; statistical digests. In addition, there is a requirement to provide the relevant specialized academic and educational guides: university calendars; lists of research in progress; lists of research organizations; yearbooks of learned societies. Rather like material for undergraduates, this area of provision is also straightforward; any professionally-trained librarian finds it a fairly simple matter to determine and obtain the works required. Reference books tend to be books which buy themselves; it is not usually difficult to decide whether a particular purchase is worthwhile; the chief restriction above a certain limit is a financial one. The reality and importance of the other category indicated by Randall and Goodrich— that category of books which supports the library's general function— should not be underestimated. One can sometimes overstress the purposiveness of a university library. As a general statement of principle one can applaud Woledge and Page's remark that ' the university library has no justification for its existence save in so far as it aids the work of the university '. But the other side of the argument must not be overlooked that a university and a university community have a cultural and educational responsibility and interest over and above their many and various specialized studies. J Periam Danton, in his article *The subject specialist in national and university libraries*, points out with regard to the idea of absolute and specific purposiveness that

' the argument, if carried to its logical conclusion, would suggest that the library of a university having neither teaching nor research programs in Russian, English literature, or Israeli studies would be justified in failing to acquire a Russian dictionary, the *Cambridge bibliography of English literature,* or the *Jewish encyclopedia.* A good university library is much more than the sum of the current bibliographical needs of its professors and students '. However, even Danton is pushing logic too far here, because as noted earlier, the three works he cites would appear in any academic library as reference tools. Nevertheless, the point he is making is an essentially valid one; and a further argument to support it was that mentioned in the section in chapter I on the functions of a university library: that a university library also has a role to play as part of its local community, where it will inevitably be regarded as an important centre of general culture and learning.

Yet another analysis of the stock of a university library is provided in the Parry Report. Here the analysis is by type of material, as follows:

' (a) students' texts;
  (b) books currently published;
  (c) series;
  (d) currently published periodicals;
  (e) rare books and manuscripts;
  (f) general desiderata including back sets of periodicals; and
  (g) other materials—
    (i) maps;
    (ii) sheet music;
    (iii) microforms;
    (iv) recorded sound on tapes or records;
    (v) cine films and other visual aids; and
    (vi) cards and tapes for computers '.

Wilson and Tauber note some further types: dissertations and theses; archives; and ' printed materials in unusual form ' (broadsides, playbills and the like). The Parry Report's type (a) will be treated more fully in the section on undergraduate collections which follows. Types (b) and (c) are self-explanatory. The problems attaching to type (d), currently published periodicals, have already been discussed, in Chapter I. Type (e) is dealt with more fully later in this chapter, in the section on special collections. Type (f) includes specific mention of back sets of periodicals; again these can account for a good deal of expenditure, especially in recently-established university libraries, though it must be remembered that a large part of the demand for these can be met by the loan and photocopy facilities offered by the British Library Lending Division. Finally, type (g) requires little comment except to note that there still remains amongst library users a good deal of resistance to microforms. As the Association of University Teachers commented in *The university library*: 'Most readers do not like microfilms as substitutes for books'—and 'The general attitude of readers to microfilms is resignation or even hostility. It is of no use for browsing'. Similarly, R E Ellsworth comments in his paper *Libraries, students. and faculty* (in the Cornell Library Conference volume): 'A motion-picture reel in a metal container, a microfilm, microcard, or microfiche of a book . . . are of no use to a scholar on the prowl'. Steven Muller in the same volume talks equivocally of the 'eye-straining magic of microfilm'.

UNDERGRADUATE COLLECTIONS

It has already been noted that the provision of undergraduate text-books is, relatively speaking, neither very expensive nor very difficult. It is nevertheless very important. The needs of undergraduates are stressed not only in the Parry Report ('We recognize that the needs of undergraduates demand special attention and that their work is certain to suffer if library facilities are inadequate'—paragraph 142), but also by the Association of University Teachers in *The university library*, which pointed out the necessity of providing 'supplementary collections of additional copies of essential textbooks' in view of the change from public lecture to 'the more intimate seminar'.

Just how many copies of a particular undergraduate textbook should be bought, and just how big such undergraduate collections should be, have, however, been the subject of some debate. Christine M Shaw in her survey of *Duplicate provision for undergraduates* comes out in favour of providing multiple copies of undergraduate texts, but she does report the experience of the undergraduate library at Glasgow University as follows: 'In carrying out previous policy, multiple

54

copies of ancillary required reading were bought immediately up to a maximum of six per title. In 1969 all these copies were examined and allocated to one of three categories: never used, never used in the current session and used in the current session. Many titles fell into the first two categories, and policy was changed as a result. Copies are now bought only in response to observed demand; one or two copies are usually bought initially, and extra ones are bought later if a demand for them can be assessed, usually in the form of reservations '. It is a common conclusion of those with experience of undergraduate collections that lecturers' assessments of student reading tend to be unreliable, and that ' observed demand ' is the only real criterion.

Carmack and Loeber, in their article *The library reserve system—another look,* also comment on the ' rather substantial gap between the teaching methods of the professor and what the student reveals to be his study habits '. Their concern is with the number of titles—the actual size of the collection—rather than with the number of copies. They examined the titles held in the reserve book system at the University of Nebraska in view of the immense amount of work involved in dealing each term with the lists of books for inclusion in the reserve system submitted by teaching departments, and found that: ' The total number of books which did not circulate during the year seems to indicate that there is a correlation between the number of titles on a reserve list and the number of times that a title circulates . . . the percentage of titles never circulated rises rather sharply for lists longer than twenty titles. On the average, of lists with 1-20 titles, 33 percent never circulated. However, of lists with 21 or more titles, 42 percent never circulated '. As a consequence of these findings, reserve lists were limited to twenty titles per course.

There remains one further debate in the matter of providing an undergraduate collection, but it is a major one. This is whether the collection, along with generous accommodation for its use, should be offered as a facility quite separate from the remainder of the library. On the whole, very few British university librarians favour an entirely separate building for undergraduate library facilities; the majority however do accept the idea of a separate area within the main building. There are many reasons for this. The chief one is the almost universal feeling that an undergraduate, even though he apparently may need basically to use only a certain, limited number of texts, should be exposed and have ready and convenient access to everything else the library has to offer. The Parry Report confirms that undergraduate collections actually stimulate, rather than discourage, use by students of the main collection. The other advantage of this by now common compromise of providing separate undergraduate facilities within the main building is that the student is thereby largely spared the quite genuine overwhelming and confusing effects of an unavoidable and premature confrontation with a very large, research-orientated library. Another point is that the actual administration of providing extra copies of students' texts is made very much simpler if such collections are annexed from the rest of the library's stock.

A quite usual arrangement now is to make the undergraduate collection a reserve book collection, whereby undergraduate texts are all kept together in a strictly-controlled area (either a special room, or a grilled area of stack) in which reading accommodation is not provided but from which students may borrow a limited number of books (up to three, say) for use anywhere in the library for a strictly limited period of time (two, or three, hours). Observation, however, does reveal that many students, having borrowed from such a collection, tend in fact to sit down at the tables nearest the collection, which plainly points to the need to include an adequate amount of seating provision in the immediate vicinity of a collection of undergraduate texts if this is at all possible.

The key to whether an undergraduate collection should be in an altogether separate building (as at Glasgow University, for example) appears to be size of university. Ralph Ellsworth in his paper on *User needs and the philosophy of the library* in *Planning the academic library* (edited by H Faulkner Brown), talking of undergraduate libraries, commented that: 'With universities of 10,000, 15,000, 20,000 or 30,000 as there are in the States, these are essential, but in Britain there are very few universities of that size, the average size is 3,000 or 4,000. It may go up in the fairly near future to 6,000 or 7,000, but at what stage does the separate undergraduate library become necessary? It is difficult to answer that accurately. When universities have about 10,000 students, something around that figure in a State university (not a private one because in some of the private ones like Princeton or Washington University, they do not need these separate facilities because there is a homogeneity of background of the students) and in a multi-purpose " Robbins " university, the critical point would seem to be somewhere between 6,000 to 10,000 and closer to 10,000 students. When Colorado got to that size, the situation began to get out of hand. It was impossible to keep the books in the stacks in any kind of order with that number of people using them. Also when the library grows to above a million books, then you begin to get into this kind of problem. So somewhere around 6,000 to 10,000 students and around a million books would seem to be the break-point '.

BOOKSHOPS

In his article *Book selection in the university library,* Pafford states that a university library should provide for undergraduates a ' well-selected modern, general, non-specialized ' collection, but one which excludes textbooks. Pafford's view is that students should buy their own textbooks, a view which is no longer accepted. Textbooks can be very expensive in some subjects; in some cases the period of their use is very limited; sometimes only parts of certain textbooks need to be consulted; very often the need for some of them is only peripheral. Thus, though a student must be encouraged to buy a reasonable number of the texts he needs, he can never be expected to obtain all of them. The problem, however, is that many students seem unwilling to buy even this reasonable proportion. A good deal of the Parry Report is concerned with discussing how to make such purchases obligatory, and it recommends that in order to ensure that students spend their local authority book grants properly ' a voucher system, with adequate safeguards, should be introduced as soon as possible '.

The Parry Report makes the obvious point that the very proximity of a bookshop encourages students to buy their own textbooks. Most universities are plainly aware of this: without exception, all of the newer universities (the majority of which are distant from a town centre) have introduced a commercially-run bookshop on to their campus. In some universities, the bookshop is actually under the

57

main library's roof. The presence of a bookshop on the university site obviously benefits the library itself, and the academic staff, as well as the students. In addition to a bookshop, students are often able to make use of a secondhand textbook service run by their union.

Students usually have sources other than the main university library from which to obtain the books they cannot buy for themselves. In some universities, there are college or halls of residence libraries. The functions of such libraries are expounded in the Parry Report, as follows:

' (a) the duplication of some of the services given by a good main library in the university; and

(b) the provision of those services which are not normally provided in a university library.'

By (a) is meant principally the provision of textbooks; and by (b) the provision of recreational and general reading matter. The most elaborate system of halls of residence libraries is that which exists at Nottingham University. This has been described in Alison Marsh's article *The library in the university hall of residence*. It was decided in 1952 to develop libraries in Halls of Residence as a matter of university library policy in Nottingham. Each of the five Halls was to have 5,000 books. Small collections already existed in some of the Halls, but they had developed haphazardly, largely as a result of gifts, and consisted mostly of out-of-date textbooks; there were no funds for their maintenance, they were poorly catalogued and they were little-used.

Nottingham decided to aim for ' browsing ' libraries, to promote the students' general education, and to exclude textbooks. Each Hall now has a separate library room, comfortably and informally equipped, and each receives an annual grant from the university library's budget. Though the main lines of policy for Halls libraries are laid down by the university library committee, each Hall has a student library committee which meets under the chairmanship of the warden. A member of the university library staff usually attends such meetings. Responsibility for book selection and for the general development of the collections rests with the Deputy Librarian, in consultation with the wardens and student committees. The students themselves look after the libraries, but the ordering and processing of new books is done centrally by a qualified assistant librarian in charge of all Halls libraries.

DEPARTMENTAL LIBRARIES

Another source of books for a student can be his or her departmental library, though this is by no means the prime function of such a library. As the *First report* of the Cambridge General Board's Committee on Libraries puts it succinctly: ' It is certain that, as a matter of historical development, the prime motive behind the creation of most departmental libraries was the provision of research material for senior academic staff in order that they might have such material immediately at hand, without the necessity of going to the university library '. What has also happened to a lesser, but varying, extent is the provision by such libraries of facilities and materials for students. The recommendation of the Cambridge Report, incidentally, was that the departmental libraries in that university should take on themselves the major burden of undergraduate provision and leave the university library free to concentrate solely on provision for research.

On the whole, British university librarians do not encourage the creation of departmental libraries. The reasons for their attitude can be readily summarized:

1) The aim in any university should be to provide a central, comprehensive collection of books and journals, freely available for long periods.

2) Such a central collection can be supervised and maintained more effectively than a departmental collection, both in respect of reader guidance and in plain security.

3) Very few subjects are of interest only to one set of people; indeed, most subjects overlap departmentally, and many overlap between faculties. Consequently, it is wrong that one department should have sole use of materials which are of interest to other sections of the university community.

4) If it is accepted that it is wrong that unique items should be

held in a departmental library, it follows that all items there should be second copies of main library titles. This therefore entails a considerable degree of wasteful duplication.

5) Departmental libraries similarly lead to wasteful duplication in respect of administration, staffing, processing and accommodation.

University librarians tend to make two exceptions to this basic attitude. The first is that they do acknowledge the need for departments to possess small collections of what may be called 'benchbooks'—that is, works to which frequent and essential reference must be made. The second exception is where a department is so geographically distant from the main collection that sheer convenience demands a separate library facility.

The Parry Report is more generous in its attitude to departmental libraries. While accepting fully that 'the university library is the heart of the university' and must be stocked and maintained as such, the report points out that there is a real 'necessity for conserving the time and energies of both staff and students' and that departmental libraries 'are an effective method of meeting that need'. The Parry committee go further, and state quite bluntly that they regard such libraries 'as recognised features of the academic library system'. Their point is a valid one: departmental libraries do have a genuine amenity value, because of their very proximity to those who teach and study in a particular subject field; and they can be more effective to readers because they do present a limited, compact and specialized collection as opposed to a large and diffused one.

The essential requirement does seem to be that the central collection must always be regarded as having first priority; it must never be weakened or deprived by irresponsible investment in departmental collections. But once that priority is met, departmental libraries can be regarded more positively than Woledge and Page's dismissal of them as 'at best but a necessary evil'. The AUT pamphlet on *The university library*, having remarked that many university teachers regard departmental libraries as being 'essential to the process of encouraging undergraduates to read intensively in their subject', goes on to make the important provisos that such collections should be:

60

1) ' carefully integrated with the main collection ';

2) ' confined to essential works of reference and multiple copies of text books which are prescribed reading for lecture courses ';

3) ' carefully supervised by the main library staff ';

4) ' catalogued by the main library ';

5) ' available to all readers in any subject or faculty '.

The Parry Report provides an additional list of recommendations:

' (i) Except possibly for class libraries, all libraries in the university should be under the jurisdiction of the library committee or similar library authority which will be responsible for their organisation and the regulations for their operation.

(ii) A union catalogue of the holdings of all the libraries in a university is essential and, where it does not exist, should be compiled as soon as possible.

(iii) In general, no library outside the central library should contain items which are unique in the university, unless it is large enough to justify the appointment of library staff adequate to offer services of the standard of the central library, including extended hours of opening.

(iv) Libraries not covered by (iii) above should, in general, contain only duplicates of books and periodicals in the central library.

(v) No library should be set up outside the central library unless there are sufficient funds to support both the initial purchase of its stock and its continued maintenance; it should not in any way interfere with the acquisitions policy of the central library. We appreciate that, wherever there are large and important departments (particularly scientific departments), which are a considerable way from the main library, they will require libraries, for the use of postgraduate students and senior members of staff, which contain basic works of reference and current periodicals and monographs. Their contents should be included in the university catalogue and their acquisitions policies should be discussed with the academic staff concerned.'

It may be concluded from both the AUT and the Parry Report recommendations that it is essential that the main library exercise a degree of control over departmental collections, treating them either as ' detached arms ' (in Davinson's phrase), or requiring them to operate within a given framework.

The foregoing section on departmental libraries stresses the validity of the idea of a central comprehensive collection. Fragmentation on an uncontrolled and irresponsible scale is very plainly undesirable. But it should not go unsaid that there is a school of thought which would support the division of a monolithic general library into major units. In his article on *Economics and the university library*, David Burnett writes: ' The other major desideratum apart from comprehensive stock provision is for ready access. In practice, however, this runs contrary to the unitary principle common in the library organization of British and American universities and favours the creation of relatively small departmental libraries which take the books to where the readers are rather than expecting them to come to the books. The centrifugal German pattern of strong specialist libraries attached to the departments as the focus of reading has, therefore, much to recommend it to the user, particularly in view of the highly specialized rather than synthetic nature of much research and study. Readers in each discipline have, moreover, a natural and reasonable desire not only to have ' their ' books close to hand but also to collect them together and have them arranged by a custom-built classification scheme, partly owing to the complexity of knowledge and the huge volume of all published literature and partly owing to the peculiar organization and even forms of publication which characterize the various branches of knowledge. The large, universal libraries of modern British universities do, in fact, run against the academic grain as regards their size and organization as well as ease of user access '.

Another ardent exponent of this view was Paul Buck of Harvard, who noted how a university community could rebel in the face of ' administrative centralization by edict '. Consequently, Harvard adopted a policy of ' co-ordinated decentralization ', whereby particular subject collections, or collections of particular types of material— rare books and manuscripts, undergraduate services, little-used material—were detached, and separately housed. Buck, however, was aware that such a policy is one which ' like walking a tightrope, requires alertness '. He saw that there were inevitable problems of communication between units (of which there were ninety two at Harvard in 1964); problems of duplication; and problems in connection with border-line subjects. There was also a risk that some subjects, because they did not fit neatly into any unit, might come to be neglected altogether.

J M Bruno in his article on *Decentralization in academic libraries* gives some statistics on the duplication of services and materials in a decentralized system: 'at Rutgers nearly 35 per cent of the total book fund is used to purchase duplicate materials for its various libraries'; and he quotes F H Wagman as stating that fully 30 per cent of the personnel budget of his library system was spent in staffing the many branches 'in less than adequate fashion', quite apart from the very high cost incurred by the cataloguing department. He also notes that the administrative control of libraries in a decentralized system becomes difficult, whether it is due to their number, or to geographical distances.

The arguments in support of Buck's view are like those in support of departmental libraries: such units can be more effective from the reader's point of view; and they can be more convenient. If the science departments of a university are distant from the arts departments, it is not illogical to have a separate science library (as at Nottingham and Durham). In other universities, historical rather than geographical reasons have caused the growth of separate major units—a medical school with its separate medical library is a very familiar situation. Also, there are subjects which do tend to be self-contained—a separate law library is equally common. However, though Bruno agrees that there is great value in 'the specialized service afforded scholars who use these collections', the argument can be double-edged in that the very dispersal of materials all over a campus can cause 'possible user frustration'.

One definite move now in decentralized systems which Bruno mentions is to consolidate small units into larger and larger divisions: to assemble a Social Sciences Library, or a Science Library, out of the various departmental libraries, for example. Of course, parallel to this kind of development is the current tendency in university libraries to prefer to have a series of major subject divisions rather than one massive general collection.

Though it is difficult to support Buck and Burnett with any great enthusiasm, as British university libraries grow in scale the idea of one indivisible whole must not go unquestioned, and should be amenable to historical, geographical and legitimate user demands.

LITTLE-USED MATERIALS

One category of material which Buck singled out in his support of a policy of decentralization was little-used material, for as Ellsworth in his Cornell Library Conference paper says wryly: 'We librarians must now make frequency counts of use and we must retire our less lively books to cheap storage warehouses, either on the outer edge of our campuses, or in some nearby city . . . For each new book we bring in an old one must go out either to storage or to be reduced to microform, or possibly to be shelved on its fore-edge, with its head down, symbolic of its uselessness, so that it will occupy less space on the shelf '.

The problems of first identifying, and then relegating, little-used materials is not of course a new one. As far back as 1901, Charles Eliot, the President of Harvard University, observed that since during the course of one year only 63,673 books had been borrowed from a library collection of 367,000 volumes, he was obliged to infer that the collection must contain a large mass of unused, or very little used, material. He therefore proposed that the Harvard bookstacks be examined every five or ten years, and those books which had not been loaned at all should be stored in a more compact manner somewhere else.

In two recent papers, Carol Seymour has reviewed research done on identifying obsolete stock. She starts by pointing out that it is not just shortage of space which demands the identification and relegation of obsolete material. 'Obsolete' material as such may have no intrinsic value, and indeed its presence on open shelves may hinder readers from finding 'live ', that is, still useful, material.

She goes on to mention the work of Richard Trueswell, who reported that 'in two libraries at Northwestern University 25 percent and 40 percent respectively of the correct collections at the two libraries would satisfy more than 99 percent of current circulation requirements '. She mentions also the work of Geoffrey Ford, who argues that too many librarians aim for size, whereas in fact they should be aiming for quality—and therefore since their aim is to build up collections, to weed would seem to defeat their purpose.

Carol Seymour notes that a librarian has to balance two things: the decreased availability of a book (if stored, transferred, or discarded), against the benefits gained—more space, a more up-to-date collection. She also notes that storing, transferring or discarding are costly in themselves, in that they require the alteration of records, and the actual removal of the books.

Coming to the criteria used for assessing the usefulness of books, she refers to the fact that while some university libraries apply qualitative criteria, the most recent emphasis has been on two quantitative criteria—past circulation, and date of publication.

It is difficult to see how a system based on qualitative criteria, whereby each academic department would confer with the library staff regarding the weeding of those parts of the collection with which it was concerned, could ever really be effective or efficient on a large scale. Within any given university the variation between the library-mindedness of different departments is enormous. Some departments use every facility the library can offer; others do not exist as far as the library is concerned. Even within active departments, it is usually a particular individual or individuals who actually make the difference in this respect. Therefore it is virtually impossible to mount a systematic, comprehensive and consistent weeding programme based on departmental co-operation. The library staff will always carry the main burden. This being the case, the preference for quantitative criteria is understandable.

As Carol Seymour records, Fussler and Simon, in their investigations into the patterns of use of books in large research libraries, found that past use was the best predictor of future use. Richard Trueswell, mentioned earlier, came to a similar conclusion: ' In one of his sample areas, 11 percent of the books in circulation had been used at least once in the previous month, 97 percent had been borrowed last within the three years previous to the sampling, and 99 percent had circulated at least once in the previous eight years. He therefore postulated that if 99 percent were the desired satisfaction rate, all books which had not circulated within the past eight years could be removed from the active collection with little loss in satisfaction to the users.

The second of Carol Seymour's articles is concerned with serials, which have entirely different patterns of use from monographs. Here, citations to articles have been taken as the measure of use; and number of citations has been linked with age of the journal in formulae for predicting the age at which volumes of a journal can be weeded. Journals are so commonly used inside libraries that circulation records cannot be employed as a guide to use, as is the case with monographs.

Having identified which are the little-used materials in the collection, a library's next step is to store them. However, Ralph Ellsworth in his book *The economics of book storage in college and university libraries* does have some cautionary remarks to say on this matter: ' To gain proper perspective on the book storage problem, one must realize that in most large university or research libraries the book collections occupy somewhat less than half of the floor space in the library building. The remainder is occupied by readers, staff, and service functions.

' It is also necessary to know that the annual cost of providing space for the book collection and for servicing it (including the cost of the land, the building, and equipment, amortized over a 50-year period, as well as maintenance and servicing of the building) represents only a very small part of a library's annual budget (only about 1 percent at one institution, MIT).

'. . . An institution, unless it is willing to use record-changing systems that are thought by many university librarians to be unacceptable, will not, if it counts all the real costs, be able to save very much money by removing a substantial number of little-used books from the bookstacks and storing them elsewhere; and at this same time it runs the risk of alienating the goodwill of some of its faculty and graduate students by lowering the quality of access to its collections. In addition, it might be creating conditions that could, in the long run, increase costs that might be much larger than are the short-term savings it might make by adopting a storage program '.

One storage possibility is that of a co-operative storage centre, on the American pattern. The first ever was the New England Deposit Library, opened in 1942, and which by 1960 was storing material for eleven Boston-based libraries, five of them college or university libraries, Harvard being the largest. The costs of running the New England Deposit Library are shared by the member libraries, each of which shelves its own material there and each of which can recall such material at any time.

Likewise, the Hampshire Inter-Library Center, set up in 1951, services four libraries all within easy reach of each other. Its original aim was to concern itself with periodicals, and to combine the research resources of members. Material deposited in the centre has first to be approved by all the member libraries, and when approved becomes the property of the centre and cannot be recalled permanently.

A third deposit library, the Mid-West Inter-Library Center, set up in 1950-51, was altogether more ambitious, with twenty members, eighteen of them universities. It has since developed from being a regional deposit for scarce, little-used research material, to a national organization—renamed Center for Research Libraries in 1964—concerned with the acquisition, presentation and dissemination of knowledge.

Neither the New England Deposit Library nor the Mid-West Inter-Library Center has achieved the major economies in storage and processing costs which were hoped for, and the conclusion seems to be that though the idea of a co-operative deposit centre for little-used materials is probably sound, it does require the application of firm and prudent policies and criteria, and that the justification for, and the possibilities of, such a centre go far beyond purely economic considerations. Joanne Harrar has observed: ' From the individually maintained storage facility to the storage unit jointly owned and operated by several libraries would seem superficially at least, a logical, economical and widely adopted transition. Yet co-operative storage, although the subject of a lengthy history and a voluminous literature, has been limited in realization . . . examples of co-operative storage enterprises undertaken on any appreciable scale have totalled only three in number.' Joanne Harrar in fact produced a dissertation on the proposed and actual benefits contributed by these three centres, but discovered that they had not halted the need for building extensions to the contributing libraries, nor had they reduced processing costs in the long-term, and nor had they eliminated unnecessary duplication.

There has been little need in Britain so far to debate the merits or otherwise of co-operative storage ventures. This is because in contrast with America's large and affluent libraries, university collections in this country average approximately only 400,000 volumes with only Oxford and Cambridge possessing in excess of 2,000,000 volumes. The need to seek additional storage space is therefore in no way so acute. The only example here is the University of London's Library Depository at the Royal Holloway College at Egham in Surrey which has been in operation since 1961. This conforms with Ellsworth's idea of a ' warehouse ' for the University of London's fifty or so libraries, and is equipped with work rooms, loading spaces, office accommodation and a room for a catalogue and a few readers. The venture has been described by the libraries concerned as no more than a useful aid, and not a particularly cheap one at that. Neither has it been conducive to convenience, as evidenced by the following comment in the Annual Report for 1971/72 of the Librarian of the British Library of Political and Economic Science; ' Pressure on space continued relentlessly, and further transfers of volumes of periodicals were made to the University Depository at Egham. Towards the end of the summer term, however, it became evident that further transfers of periodicals would only aggravate an already difficult situation, for during the session 3,349 volumes had to be brought back for use in the library (had to be sent for, recorded, separately housed and serviced for varying periods, and eventually returned)'.

The Parry Committee made the following four main recommendations about such depositories:

i) the material deposited should be limited to categories which conform to a very strict interpretation of the description ' little-used ';

ii) the material deposited should be ' easily retrievable ';

iii) ' bibliographical control should be of the simplest, otherwise expenditure will mount '; and

iv) the provision of reader accommodation in such depositories must be regarded as being of secondary importance.

This list of specifications would fit in very neatly with the proposed

68

role of the British Library as a depository. The Yorkshire wing of that organization, at Boston Spa, has already indicated its willingness to establish some kind of clearing-house for material whose level of use creates storage problems for other libraries.

Another storage possibility is the use of microforms, though these ought not to be regarded solely as a form of miniaturization to save space. True enough, as Rolland E Stevens has said, one can and should replace large, bulky volumes such as newspaper volumes with a compact form that is easier to handle and to use, and one can replace other printed sources with copies in microform in order to save stack space; but additionally, there are three other reasons: '1) to obtain rare books, journals, manuscripts, archives, and other needed information sources that are either unobtainable or prohibitively expensive in their original form; 2) to replace items that are printed or written on badly deteriorating paper; 3) to furnish a working copy of rare and fragile books '. Of course, if one proposes to supply one's users with a great deal of material in microform, one must provide the complete package: sufficient and appropriate microform readers, and a reader-printer service.

SPECIAL COLLECTIONS

All university libraries have a number of what are termed special collections. These are special in the sense that they are self-contained collections, quite separate in every way from the library's ordinary bookstock. Usually they have come to the library as a gift or bequest. In character, they are more often than not concerned with a particular subject—the French Revolution collection at Nottingham, for example, or the history of early medicine and zoology collection at Reading— or with a particular type of publication—again, for example, the children's literature collections at both Nottingham and Reading. As gifts and bequests, they also usually have the characteristic that they were once private collections, and generally continue to bear the name of their original owner—for example, the Parkes Library at Southampton, which is concerned with Jewish studies.

University libraries tend to be proud of such special collections. They add a distinctive flavour to what would otherwise be a very workaday bookstock. Woledge and Page point out other merits: that such collections act as magnets for other gifts and bequests; that they are of great value to scholars in the particular subject field; that they appeal to the 'collecting instinct' of the library staff; and that they encourage the staff to pursue 'bibliographical studies' based on them.

There is, however, a justification for a library accepting such collections which is more basic than any of these. The justification is that every library has a repository function, the responsibility to act as the keeper (in Archibald Macleish's words) of 'the records of the human spirit'. There is nothing fanciful about such a view: all librarians are custodians. Where problems do arise is in connection with the responsibilities of housing such collections and in expenditure on them.

If a special collection is offered to a university library as an outright gift or bequest, the librarian is usually able to accept it. Because of the library's repository role, it is not particularly relevant whether the content of the collection has any immediate connection with the university's current teaching and research programme, though a magnanimous librarian should always be willing to suggest in some cases a more obviously appropriate library than his own for a particular collection. What is relevant is whether the library can house the collection without causing serious adjustments and dislocations of its storage and shelving capacities, whether the expense and effort of processing and cataloguing it is justified by its intrinsic value, and whether the library's funds will stretch to covering the costs of maintaining and adding to it. For these reasons it is important also that the librarian be wary of any restrictive conditions attached to particular collections: for example, that the books in it must be kept in locked cases, or their use impossibly limited.

When it is a matter not of the gift or bequest, but of the purchase of a special collection, the debate is a much harder one. Very few libraries could contemplate such a purchase unless the particular collection had a specific relevance to the university's teaching or research needs. Library funds are nowhere so liberal. This even comes down sometimes to having to calculate just what percentage of a collection is relevant: often a library has need of a number of items in a collection which is offered for purchase, but has to refuse the offer because the purchase of the whole is demanded.

Linked with the above kind of debate, is the question of buying rare books. As the Parry Report comments: 'It is not proper to subsidise from public funds a desire to acquire items simply because they are bibliographical curiosities'. This cannot really be contested; and there was certainly an unfortunate tendency in university libraries during their 'storehouse' period of development to indulge in this type of acquisition, which in merit ranks no higher than collecting postage stamps. But 'bibliographical curiosities' apart, there are many valid reasons why a university library must acquire rare books. As the Parry Report also says, such books are essential for many sorts of research: first editions for the establishing of definitive literary texts, for example; or rare political pamphlets, which are raw materials of history. Again too, there is the library's function as custodian and repository: it is every library's duty to share in the preservation and retention of the important printed records of man's achievements.

Even when a library has acquired rare items, it is becoming increasingly difficult at the present time to preserve and retain them. Book thefts from libraries are no new thing, but the sharp rise in recent years of the value of rare books has led to a notable increase in this kind of crime. In January 1972 a conference on the problem of theft was held under the aegis of the Antiquarian Booksellers' Association and the Rare Books Group of the Library Association, and on the recommendation of that meeting a Working Party was set up to prepare a report. The report recommended that access to books of value in libraries should be more rigorously restricted; that libraries should mark all valuable books and documents in such a way as to be both a deterrent to thieves and a warning to a prospective buyer that a book or document has been stolen; and that a list of stolen books be prepared by the Antiquarian Booksellers' Association and distributed under the joint imprint of the ABA and the Library Association.

Apart from special collections in the sense of self-contained collections of books outside the ordinary range of a library's bookstock, there are also collections which are special in the sense that they comprise non-book materials: maps, gramophone records, music, archives, manuscripts, and others as listed in the preliminary section of this chapter. They are consequently special in the ways in which their particular form has to be housed and administered. A map collection requires map cabinets rather than conventional shelving, light tables and large consultation surfaces rather than the standard furniture offered elsewhere in the library; it demands a different method of cataloguing and classification; it has different regulations for its use; it needs a specialist curator to look after it. The same is true of a gramophone record collection, or a music collection, or any other, the actual type and nature of the material in each case dictating how it needs to be handled and accommodated.

Manuscript and archive collections are of particular interest. The material held in university libraries normally falls into three categories: university archives; records of private firms, institutions and societies; and literary and personal papers.

The responsibility a library has to its university has been repeatedly stressed in this book: the same responsibility covers an obligation to help in the preservation of the university's archives. These comprise the official correspondence, minutes, and books of account of the university's administration; publications of the university (especially of the university press, if any); books by and about staff and students of the university; theses by past and present members of the university; records of university clubs, associations and societies (especially the students' representative council); news cuttings and ephemera; personal papers of the more eminent members of the staff; and paintings, photographs and busts relating to the university. Material of this kind is normally collected for two reasons: (i) because of its value for the history of the university and of higher education generally; and (ii) because of its continuing value for current administration. Although university archives are perhaps most often preserved in the university library, as at Reading University for example, this is not a universal rule. At the University of Liverpool, the University Archivist is an officer of the Registrar's department and his collections are kept in the Registrar's repository. The functions of the university's archivist, whether based in the university library or not, are to ensure

i) the prompt destruction of useless and unwanted university records;

ii) the temporary preservation of records which need to be kept by the university only for a limited time; and

iii) the indefinite preservation within the university of permanently valuable records.

The second category of material, the records of private firms, institutions and societies, usually relate to some part of the teaching and research work of the university. Thus the Library of the London School of Economics holds records of trade unions; Reading University holds records of publishing, printing, and farming; and King's College, London, has a Centre for Military Archives. Such collections arise directly from studies pursued in the respective universities.

The third category of material, literary and personal papers, again often reflect parts of the curriculum or the research interests of the university staff; or they have some strong local association. Sometimes, of course, they arise from entirely fortuitous gifts or bequests. If, however, it can be shown that the literary and personal papers kept in a specific university library represent collections of national importance, for example, those of the Webbs in the London School of Economics or of the Chamberlain family in the University of Birmingham, then the library is justified in acquiring by purchase or gift as many related items as possible. There is also a case for the purchase by university libraries of literary and personal papers offered in sale rooms, if it seems likely that they would otherwise fall into private hands and thus be less easily accessible. Perhaps the soundest principle to follow in the acquisition of papers in this category is that the papers should reflect some significant and lasting element in the teaching and research of the university, especially if this element is unique to the university. The prestige motive by itself should be avoided.

Increasingly, universities are appointing to the library staff librarians and archivists with experience in arranging, storing and describing manuscripts. This is a good sign if it means that existing collections of long standing are to be properly treated. But such appointments should ideally be made, not when collections have been accumulating for some years, but when they are begun. No university library should embark on an ambitious scheme for gathering records and manuscripts or university archives without engaging a trained person to take charge of it.

In a general way, the basic issues which guide a library's book selection policy have already been treated in this and in preceding chapters. The main point is that a university library services its own university community. If a university does not have a teaching or research programme in Russian studies, there is no justification for the library buying Russian materials: though it has been made equally clear that the library, in its general role as part of a centre of culture and learning, would still need to have, for example, the works of Tolstoy, and a standard history of Russia. The analyses of stock earlier in this chapter have defined just as plainly some incontestable needs: undergraduate provision, reference provision. Selection policies regarding departmental libraries and halls of residence libraries have also been treated; and the case presented for the acquisition of special collections and rare books.

The section on finance in the first chapter described the common arrangement in British university libraries whereby most of a library's book-fund is divided up between academic departments: it follows as a consequence of this that the basic task of apportionment and balance of stock rests in the librarian's hands only to the extent that he recommends what the various departmental allocations should be, subject to the approval of his library committee. How these departmental allocations are spent tends to be very much a departmental, rather than a library, matter, even though there may be the formality of the librarian approving every purchase—and a formality is precisely what it tends to be.

Since funds are always limited, this is in no way really improper. Poverty is the only justification for the system, but unfortunately it is a sufficient one. Only in a free, affluent situation could the librarian and his staff exercise any real control. However, whether poverty-stricken or affluent, the essential ingredient of university library book selection is the same: co-operation between the library staff and the teaching staff. It will be shown later, in the chapter on reader services, that such co-operation flourishes altogether more effectively when the library has some kind of subject specialization system. J Periam Danton in his article on *The subject specialist in national and university libraries* puts this very strongly, and argues that a subject specialist system would: '(a) ensure that the important books in all relevant fields are acquired; (b) place authority where responsibility alone now generally exists; and (c) place book selection subject to library administrative control and supervision'. In support of this view, that the main burden and responsibility for book selection must rest on the library staff, he cites a number of reasons why the present state of affairs, where the academic staff do most of the book selection, is not likely to persist: ' the remarkable increment in the pace, intensity, and activities of modern academic life which leaves most faculty members with little time or inclination for book selection; the great growth in the size and complexity of library collections and of world publishing, to the bafflement of the ' old-fashioned ', part-time faculty book selector; and, if it is chiefly poverty that makes dedicated book selectors of faculty, he becomes disinterested and unconcerned when his university library nears the million-volume figure '.

Many other librarians have argued that chief responsibility for book selection must lie with the library staff. Gelfand in *University libraries for developing countries* declares that only the librarian and his staff are sufficiently free (as opposed to teaching staff) and permanent (as opposed to students) to acquire books continuously and systematically. Pafford in his article *Book selection in the university library,* having acknowledged that book selection is basically a co-operative effort involving the teaching staff, the library staff, and all who use the library, nevertheless insists that ' book selection in all its aspects is the prime responsibility of the university librarian '—again because of his permanence and professional dedication—but also because he is aware of the total context. The Parry Report gives further reasons: only the library staff ' can be fully conversant with all aspects of the library's collection '; and the range of material to select from is now so wide (any large library now receives notification of about 350,000 new books annually) that a central selection organization is the only possible system. An obvious gloss here is that only the library can have the massive range of current and retrospective bibliographies, bibliographical handbooks and book selection tools which are needed for the effective performance of the task.

However, the current situation in British university libraries without subject specialization and with a fairly rigid departmental allocation system—and this is still the most common situation—does mean that the chief responsibility for book selection will continue to lie with the academic staff. What the library staff must therefore do is to liaise and advise and negotiate as vigorously as possible. A great help in such dealings is the appointment by each academic department of a departmental 'bookman' or 'library representative', through whom all departmental book requests are made, and with whom the library staff can liaise.

Any treatment of book selection cannot afford to overlook the question of periodicals. As indicated in the section on Finance in Chapter I, these undoubtedly represent the British university librarian's biggest headache as far as selection of library materials is concerned. It is obvious therefore that the selection of periodical titles must be strictly and critically controlled. The curious thing is that whereas funds for books have usually been tightly allocated according to departments, recommendations for new periodicals have been made a charge on a general periodicals fund. This system makes administrative sense, but unfortunately in many libraries at various times not enough control has been exercised on such additions. Periodicals are increasingly important and increasingly expensive: there must be a very great degree of co-operation between library and academic staff in their selection. There must also be more formal machinery for such co-operation. The system adopted by some older university libraries —Glasgow, for example—whereby all recommendations for new periodical titles go before a special meeting of the library committee, complete with specimen copies and letters of support from interested members of the academic staff, is tedious but extremely effective. The Glasgow system also involves the placing of any new subscription on a trial basis—for one year only, or for three years only—so that subsequently it comes back to the committee for a final review. Again this is to be commended.

Finally in this section on selection, a few remarks are merited on the idea of a 'balanced stock'. This particular catchphrase has been current for many years and has only been queried quite recently, by D J Foskett in his article *The intellectual and social challenge of the library service*. Foskett refers to it as an 'ineffable notion'—' as if the library were some kind of cake, needing exact proportions of the

1 : Visible index system of recording periodicals.

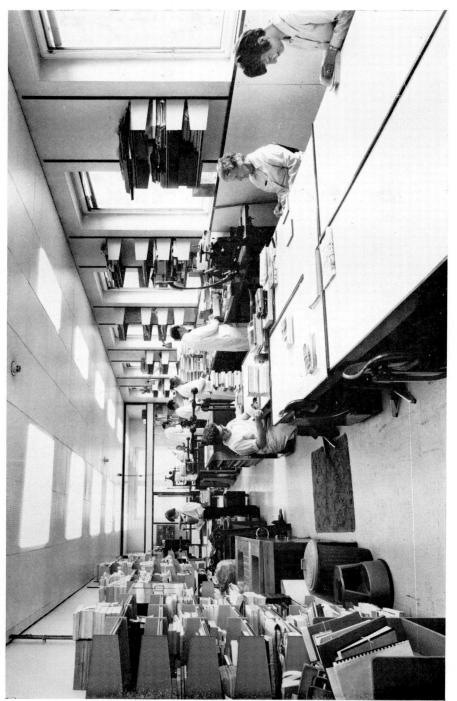

2 : Library bindery, Reading University.

3 : Book issue system, Surrey University Library.

4 : COM catalogue.

5: Entrance area, Reading University Library.

6: Old library (left) and new library (right), Glasgow University.

7: Bookstack area, Reading University Library.

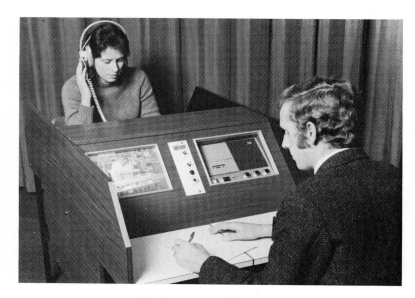

8 : Surrey tape-slide carrel.

various ingredients for success '. Certainly as far as university libraries are concerned, his debunking is at least partially justified. A degree of balance is obviously needed, but the true test of a university library's ' balance ' is in relation to the needs of the university it serves. It has very much less to do with any kind of balance within the library itself. If the university has a massive school of contemporary European studies, and a tiny philosophy department, the library will reflect this: the imbalance will not be real. In other words, a lopsided university will have a lopsided university library. It points up the real fact of life that in the last analysis it is the university, not the university's librarian, which dictates the basic shape and content of the library's stock.

SIZE OF STOCK

It was noted in the section of this chapter on little-used materials that the bookstock of the average British university library is approximately 400,000 volumes and that only Oxford and Cambridge have more than 2,000,000 volumes. It would seem therefore that any discussion of what the ultimate size of a university library bookstock should be might perhaps be premature: but in fact this issue has already been raised in a number of quarters.

Any such discussion should begin by observing that the general opinion among British university librarians is that their libraries are under-financed and under-stocked. Their opinion is supported by the AUT, which, in *The university library*, comments that existing collections, by any reasonable standard, are ' woefully inadequate '. The overall impression which the Parry Report gives is much the same : not that economies are demanded, but that further and considerable bolstering is needed.

No one really holds the view that magnitude equals excellence, and no one aspires to completeness. But there is widespread support for the view that the needs of scholarship require (in the words of the *Annual report* of the Vice-Chancellor of the University of East Anglia for 1966-7) ' regular and rapid access to a catholic collection of academic writings, both old and new '. The same report adds: ' The borrowing of large numbers of books *seriatim* from other libraries is a very poor substitute, apart from the frustration often experienced by delay and unavailability'. In connection with this last, the Parry Report also recommends that 'there should be a high percentage of immediate availability in all subject fields', though adding 'one hundred percent immediate availability would not be practicable even with unlimited funds'. A formula of sorts is offered on this point by the AUT: since all universities cannot expand at the same rate in all subjects, each should therefore develop specialized interests.

Even though national lending libraries such as the NLLST have demonstrated their efficiency as a loan service, it is obvious from the above that no matter how efficient such services are, there will always remain the need for a considerable collection of books on every university campus. Neither is there any real prospect that a substitute might develop in the form of some kind of push-button system of information retrieval, since as Ellsworth points out in his Cornell Library Conference paper, one must distinguish the 'educational' needs of scholars from their 'informational' ones.

The debate therefore returns to what in fact is the current policy of university libraries: namely, not to aim at an overall completeness, but to provide a high degree of immediate availability in those fields with which the individual university is concerned. And since universities continue to grow, university library bookstocks must grow. If a university of 5,000 students has a library stock of 400,000 volumes, and if that university aims eventually to have 8,000 students with an attendant growth in the subject fields covered and in members of academic staff, then it must also plan a university library bookstock getting on for 1,000,000 volumes. No development of national lending services or push-button retrieval systems will counteract this. The debate, however, might take a new lease of life as that 1,000,000 is approached. No librarian of a medium-sized university is likely to want to plan much beyond that stage at present. After all, on present showing, it is going to take him at least twenty years to get there.

V

PROCESSES AND ROUTINES

GENERAL ORGANIZATION: In their book *Scientific management of library operations*, Dougherty and Heinritz point out that seventy to ninety percent of all library work consists of repetitive processes and routines. The organization of such work must therefore be rigorous and critical. The managerial formula which Dougherty and Heinritz present is one which has been touched upon already, in chapter II: the constant application of the six standard questions, why? what? where? when? who? how?

Why? is an obvious question, but it is one which is too infrequently asked. Something continues to be done because, in library memory, it always has been done. Dougherty and Heinritz remind us that the primary object of management is the 'elimination of unnecessary operations', and suggests that if in respect to a particular library routine no convincing answer is given to that question 'is it necessary?', then the next step is to do away with that operation on an experimental basis; if nothing catastrophic happens, then the validity of the elimination is proved. The specific example of elimination which they quote concerns the common (and tedious) procedure of searching the library's shelves before sending out overdue notices: this can be dispensed with completely by the simple expedient of rewording overdue notices to the effect that 'if the patron has already returned his book, please disregard the notice'.

What? is really just another version ('what is the purpose . . .? what does it contribute . . .?') of why? But where? and when? are much more interesting questions. To answer them, there must be a sound, overall grasp of the sequence of operations. The best way to follow this sequence is to trace the route of a book through the library, from its initial recommendation for purchase to its eventual appearance on the shelves. First it must be ordered; then accessioned; then catalogued and classified; then prepared (book-plated, class-marked,

bound, and so on); then shelved. Where are these operations performed?
—are the various locations conveniently grouped? When are the
operations performed?—does each routine take place at the optimum
point in the overall time sequence? Asking the questions when? and
where? can often result in revealing an opportunity for the combination of two or more operations; and combination, as Dougherty and
Heinritz also note, is as valuable a managerial device as elimination. A
good example of this is one in respect of book ordering routines: a
title recommended for purchase has first to be checked against the
library's catalogue (to make sure that it is not in stock already), and
then in the acquisition department's ' on order ' file (to establish that
it has not already been ordered); an immediate saving results if (as
in the University of East Anglia Library, for example) ' on order'
cards are filed in the library's catalogue, so that these two checking
operations are combined into one. Asking specifically the question
when? can often result in the application of another major managerial
device: ' changing the sequence of operation '. The example given by
Dougherty and Heinritz here relates to the ordering of catalogue
cards (from the Library of Congress or from the British National
Bibliography). In many libraries this is only done when a book has
reached the cataloguing department; however, if the sequence of
operations is changed so that both catalogue cards and book are
ordered by the acquisitions department, then though there may be a
risk of receiving cards which are not needed, there is inevitably a
reduction in the time a book takes to be processed by the library.
Where? as a question, of course, has a relevance in the physical
planning of a library: the acquisitions department needs to be near
the cataloguing department which needs to be near the public catalogue, and so on.

Who? is a question to do with the economics of labour. A classic
failing in libraries is to employ highly-educated and highly-paid
personnel on routine and undemanding behind-the-scenes tasks; and
conversely, to leave vital matters such as dealing with users to the
newest of juniors. It is the university librarian's responsibility to see
that every library operation is performed by the appropriate grade of
staff; and this means he must examine every operation and assess what
it requires in the way of expertise and experience from those who

perform it. On principle, he should aim at fully stretching his staff's capabilities; he must never insult their intelligence by under-employing them, nor allow them to insult their own by over-estimating the implications of some humdrum process. It is too easy for an outsider to dismiss a librarian as somebody who ' stamps books '; it is also too easy for a librarian to rebuff this particular charge while contentedly continuing to spend most of his day on tasks which are an equally poor reflection of his intellectual and professional attainment. Dougherty and Heinritz consequently add to elimination, combination, and changing the sequence of operations, this further managerial device: changing the operator.

The remaining question is, how? This involves examining and analyzing every library routine, seeking always a better (and probably simpler) way of doing things. In many cases this may mean replacing or supplementing human resources by various pieces of equipment. For example, the accounting side of library procedures surely demands at least an adding machine; and better still, a computerized system. The process is inevitable: the invention of the typewriter invalidated the use of the quill pen. Libraries must take advantage of every technical device which is relevant to their work. Cost does come into it, and gimmickry for gimmickry's sake must be avoided; but the balance of error in libraries still lies on the side of using solely human resources on tasks which could be readily eased by the introduction of appropriate equipment.

In addition to these six specific questions, some more general considerations must be borne in mind in the organization of processes and routines. The first is that there will always be a degree of resistance to change. Change demands effort, rethinking adjustment, risk; to leave things as they are (especially if they seem to work, or at least more or less work) is a great temptation. This means that the manager or organizer of processes and routines must have powers of persuasion as well as the ability to analyse and identify faults. If an innovation is not sufficiently explained and negotiated, its chances of success are bound to be reduced.

One element in the initial resistance to change which the organizer of processes and routines will find is what might be called professional mystique. Assistants who have performed and been solely responsible for a particular function over a long period of time are not infrequently liable to refer to and hint at intricacies and complications which only they can ever appreciate. This can have the effect of seriously hindering the introduction of any innovation, since to establish the precise specifications of a particular routine or set of routines then requires persistence and patience of a very high order, not to mention the capacity to endure what can amount to an almost psychological battle. Protection against this kind of difficulty will be obtained only if the university librarian insists on the compilation of a staff manual. A staff manual is a written, detailed account of every library routine, process and service. Its contents are provided by each departmental or section head, and are kept up-to-date by them. Such a record should provide the administrator with all the information he needs on the workings of the library. Its other obvious advantage, apart from acting as an authority file for the library staff generally, is that a newcomer to the staff can readily establish from it the details and responsibilities of any task assigned to him.

An additional protection against mystique—which in human terms usually means that what is involved in a particular job is known only to one person and is recorded only in that person's head—is to have every key position understudied. If, for example, the library accountant is assigned some sort of deputy (not necessarily a person who is usually working on the accounts also, but one in a related area—ordering, perhaps), then the library is protected from the kind of breakdown of operations which would happen if the accountant had to be absent from work for some reason or other.

COMPUTERIZATION

Computerization, or automation, is the best hope for the future organization of library processes and routines. It will be clear from the preceding section that a library's 'housekeeping' activities take up the greater part of the staff's time; secondly, that such operations by their very nature are repetitive; and lastly, that by and large these operations are clerical and fairly simple. A computer works at speed, so reducing the time involved; it is ideally suited for repetitive operations; and it can already be programmed to deal with most of a library's basic transactions. As L E Taylor comments in his article

The challenge of automation for the established university library: 'A large part of the work in a library is concerned not with books, but with records of books. We make a record of a book before it is ordered, probably quite a number of records; when it is received in the library there are more records, in the accounts section, the acquisitions section, an " in process " file, many records in different catalogues, in accessions lists, in bibliographies, and when the book is borrowed for use, a further record is made. On the accuracy of these records and the speed with which they are compiled, depends, to a large extent, the efficient functioning of the library.

'A computer is also a device whereby records are stored, combined in various ways according to instructions given to it, and the appropriate information produced as required.

'As yet, in a library, the original record must still be produced by human agency, and so remains a comparatively slow and expensive process. That being so, it would seem sensible, and not impossible, to make one master record of a book, containing all the information we are ever likely to need about the book, and feed it into the computer, which will then store it away in its memory. From a file of such master records the computer can, when properly instructed, produce any desired set of records, selecting, sorting, combining and recombining as required '.

It must be said, of course, that practically all that has been done so far in the way of computerizing library operations has been explicitly or implicitly experimental, and without doubt there have been a number of false starts. But the essential validity of the application of computers to library routines has been firmly established, particularly in large libraries. There will be changes and improvements in what is now taking place, but this is no real argument for holding back: almost any computerized system of circulation control, for example, would be better than our tedious, time-wasting and inefficient conventional systems, especially since, as R T Kimber and P Havard-Williams reported to the Standing Conference of National and University Libraries in 1968, it ' can now safely be said that satisfactory, well-proven, off-line circulation system designs exist for any library wishing to introduce one '.

Quite apart from these bread-and-butter aspects of library work, the use of computers offers even more dramatic possibilities in the way of providing access to the information which a library stores in its books, its indexes, and its catalogues, and of improving the efficiency and effectiveness of its services generally. In *The functions of a university library* (one of the papers collected in *University and research library studies*, edited by W L Saunders), M B Line sums up all the possibilities of computers in libraries, as follows: 'They can . . . help to provide access in various ways to information . . .They offer an extremely flexible way of sorting factual data, indexes and catalogue entries. They give hopes of . . . lightening necessary administrative operations such as circulation and acquisition systems. They make it possible to analyse the whole operational system and to provide the basis for optimization of library services and for better decision-making at various levels.' However, like many other librarians involved in the study of computer applications, Line recommends wariness as well as awareness. It is nevertheless exciting to contemplate the kind of future described in the *Report of the National Libraries Committee*: ' It is not unduly fanciful to predict that within two or three decades the larger university and public libraries, research laboratories and industrial firms will be directly linked through their individual computer terminals not only to the computerized catalogue of our national libraries, but also to other types of information service in this country and abroad. By that time, if not before, the processes of searching and locating inter-library loans will be fully computerized and direct dialogue between interrogator and computer information source may well have become commonplace. Beyond that period prediction is very uncertain, but . . . it is very likely that . . . computer storage capacity will begin to be able to cope with the retention of full texts of the world's literature, to process it in response to particular queries and, if necessary, to display it remotely by facsimile transmission wherever it is needed.'

A major factor to be considered is cost. In his article *The economic goal of library automation*, Frederick G Kilgour reports the findings of William G Bowen (in his book *The economics of major private universities*) that American private universities experienced an annual rise in cost per student of 7·5 per cent, compared with a 2 per cent increase in the general economy; he argues from this that if a crisis is to be avoided, library costs, which are going up exponentially at a frightening rate, must be brought into line with cost rises in the economy as a whole. The way this can be done, in his opinion, is by a steadily increasing rate of productivity in libraries (in cataloguing operations, for example); and the route to this increased productivity will be innovative technology, in the form of the computer. Kilgour, nevertheless, is not unaware of the considerable initial expenditure necessary, on experimental efforts, equipment, retraining of staff, and so on.

The application of computers to specific processes and routines will be dealt with in the relevant sections of the remainder of this chapter and in the next, but a brief overall survey of some of the things which are happening in the various areas of operation may be useful here. A fuller survey is supplied by R M Duchesne and A B Phillips in their article *Automation activities in British university libraries*, based on questionnaires circulated to 62 libraries (61 replying) in October/November 1970 by the Aslib Computer Applications Group on behalf of Aslib, SCONUL and the National Libraries ADP Study. Duchesne and Phillips found that: ' The broad picture presented is of widespread mechanization of the housekeeping rather than the information retrieval type. Over 60 percent of libraries had one or more applications . . . The amount of effort going into library automation is formidable, equivalent to the effort of (very approximately) fifty full-time persons divided roughly equally between library staff and system analysts/programmers '.

Computers were originally developed to handle numerical data, and therefore an obvious application has been to ordering and accounting procedures. The City University has operated since November 1967 a computerized system of library accounts which provides an alphabetical list of booksellers showing the business transacted to date with each, a list of bookfunds and the orders charged against them, and analyses of expenditure both by category (that is, books, journals, binding, and so on) and by book fund. C L Stevenson and J A Cooper describe the system in their article *A computerised accounts system at the City University*. The basic programme for this operation was subsequently adapted to listing furniture and equipment for City University's new library building (see B J Enright

85

and J A Cooper's article *The housekeeping of housekeeping: a library furniture and equipment inventory programme*). The University of Newcastle, since Easter 1966, has operated a computerized system of book ordering (which will be described more fully in the section on ordering and accessioning which follows), but here the emphasis is on the mechanics of ordering rather than on the purely accounting side. Manchester University Library has had a computerized acquisitions system in experimental operation since January 1971 (described by C J Hunt in his article in *Program*). Under an OSTI grant, the Universities of Southampton and Loughborough are working to complete a detailed specification for an ordering and accounting system and to key it into a cataloguing system using BNB MARC records (more information about which follows in the section on cataloguing).

The University of Southampton's speciality in the field of computerization has been in the area of circulation control, and the system used will be described in detail in the next chapter; but an ever-growing number of other university libraries are venturing into this same area, though not necessarily on the same lines.

The computerization of periodicals records has been another (and difficult) area of venture. The Bodleian Library has already published the first stage of a union list of scientific periodicals, and on the basis of the paper tape punched as a by-product of this, will by means of a computer be able to update this first stage, extend it, and select from it departmental lists. Brunel University has replaced its card catalogue for serials with a list kept and maintained on tape, from which many print-outs can easily be made; and from the main list special subject lists and a union list of serials have been developed (see R W P Wyatt's article, *Producing a serials catalogue on tape*). At the City University, work is going on to produce a periodicals checking-in system, the idea being to have the computer print a list of those periodical parts which are expected each month, against which a manual check can be made: the ultimate aim being to automate this part of the operation also. At Loughborough, in conjunction with the Birmingham Libraries Co-operative Mechanization Project, there is being developed a system called MASS (MARC-based Automated serials system, a serials format paralleling MARC.

86

Computerized cataloguing has come to mean almost exclusively the Library of Congress MARC project, linked in this country with the British National Bibliography. Again supported by OSTI, a network of libraries (including Southampton, Loughborough and the Bodleian) will be using the first tapes on an experimental basis. There are, however, a number of independent ventures: the University of Newcastle has transferred its card catalogue on to tape; the Old Dominion Foundation has financed a pilot project (called LOC) to produce by computer a union catalogue of pre-1801 books in the Bodleian, Cambridge University and the British Museum libraries; and the Bodleian Library has undertaken on a full production basis the conversion of its pre-1920 catalogue entries to machine readable records structured for handling by computer (see Peter Brown's account, *The Bodleian catalogue as machine readable records*). Another independent venture is the City University's computer-produced subject index to the Universal Decimal Classification.

The foregoing can only be a partial survey, because now almost every major university library in Britain (as Duchesne and Phillips have found) is at least planning to computerize some part of its activities, and new developments are reported regularly. But it will be seen that a start has been made on all of the principle areas of library operations—accounting, ordering, periodicals recording, cataloguing, and circulation control.

ORDERING AND ACCESSIONING

When a book is recommended for addition to stock, the recommendation may come to the university librarian himself, or to one of the library's service points, or to one of its subject specialist staff. In each case, once the recommendation has been approved, it will be passed for action to the order (or acquisitions) department. In some libraries, recommendations are sent by the academic staff directly to the order department, but most librarians, for a variety of obvious reasons, prefer to see what is being asked for—or, at the very least, to delegate such scrutiny to their deputy librarian. Indeed, it is quite usual to find that the chief function of a deputy librarian is the general superintendence of the order department.

The long series of processes and routines to which all additions to a library's stock are subject begins in the order department. First, the bibliographical details of the book which is being recommended are verified—author, title, date, publisher, price—if the information given is insufficient or unreliable. Most order departments, though, do try to avoid unnecessary or over-elaborate checking, for expediency's sake: because rapid action is what the recommender principally requires. After such verification as is essential, the next step is for the staff of the order department to check the library's catalogue to see whether the book is already in stock: if it is, then the recommendation is returned to the recommender endorsed to that effect. If the book is not in stock, the next check must be to see whether it is already on order: if it is, again the recommender will be informed.

If the book is neither in stock nor on order, the order department will select a source of supply (usually a bookseller), and prepare and post an order for it. Part of the routine will also be to make a note of the financial commitment involved. When the book arrives, it is checked against the bookseller's invoice and against the original order; the price (and discount, if any) is checked and noted in the library's accounts; and the invoice passed to the university accounts department for payment. Finally, before the book is passed to the cataloguing department, some kind of accessions record of it is made.

The traditional ordering system comprises the following elements:

1 A card-file, alphabetically arranged by author, of books on order. The cards are prepared by the order department on the basis of ' recommendation ' forms or slips filled in by the person requesting the book. The ' on order ' cards, apart from details of the book itself, record the date ordered, the order number, the bookseller's name, and the fund to be charged.

2 A book, or set, of duplicate order forms. Each order form is headed with the library's name, and the forms are numbered consecutively. On the form is a place for the bookseller's name, and columns in which to list the details of the books being ordered.

3 An accessions register. This is a ledger in which the details (including source of supply) of each book acquired are entered against a running number (the accession number).

This system is sound, simple and effective, often very much more so than some of the variants which replaced it. Variants became necessary as the volume of business grew and the consequent need for more automatic checks on its efficiency when the memory of the orders assistant could no longer cope. One variant (at Nottingham, for example) is to use edge-punched cards for the ' on order ' file. When the standard details have been written or typed on the card, the orders assistant then punches out with a small hand-punch appropriate perimeter holes representing date ordered, bookseller, and fund charged. This makes it possible, periodically, to go fairly quickly through the entire file and pick out all cards ordered at a particular time (this is necessary in chasing up tardy orders), or from a particular bookseller (for the same reason), or against a particular fund (since most university libraries provide regular expenditure accounts for each academic department as part of the standard ' allocation ' system mentioned already in this book). This picking-out process is done by inserting a knitting-needle through the relevant date (or bookseller, or fund) holes of the card-file, lifting up the cards and shaking them: the result is that those cards where the particular hole was punched out reveal themselves by falling free. The mechanics of this system obviously have some disadvantages: cards do not always fall free readily, and the file needs to be processed, rather tediously, in manageable batches rather than all at once if accurate results are to be obtained. However, the system does facilitate considerably the routine, necessary analyses of the ' on order ' file.

Sheffield uses basically the same system but employs a Kalamazoo Fact Finder sorting machine for its edge-punched cards, rather than Nottingham's more manual approach. Sheffield, however, has added a much more interesting variant in connection with the second element of the traditional ordering system, the preparation of orders to booksellers. Instead of typing the information on the order cards on to order forms for despatch to booksellers, and thereby (apart from the work involved) inevitably running the risk of typing errors, Sheffield xeroxes its order cards on to sheets; two sheets are made, one going to the bookseller as the order, the other being retained by the library as a record of the order. Sheffield have also departed from the traditional ledger-type of accessions register: when a book is received, the original order card is given a number and transferred to another file; this file, kept in accession number order, constitutes Sheffield's accessions record. Glasgow, in this same connection, retains its duplicate order forms (which are of the traditional type) as an accessions register: the accession number is a combination of the order sheet number and an item number.

East Anglia, like a number of other libraries, decided at its outset to abandon the idea of accession numbers (and therefore of any sort of accessions register). This would have distressed Woledge and Page who comment that the 'old-fashioned accessions register' gave 'in good perspective a solid-looking historical record of the growth of the library'. It is in fact doubtful whether a library can dispense with this type of record. One reason is that present computerized systems tend to depend on every item in a library having a unique number: and the obvious candidate is the accessions number. A second important reason is the current interest (mentioned in the very first chapter of this book) of the Comptroller and Auditor General: universities and university libraries have to be fully accountable, and a library's accessions record provides the kind of proof and evidence of expenditure which an auditor must have. The library's catalogue is not appropriate for this function, because it is a bibliographical tool, not an inventory or stock record. East Anglia, however, does furnish an example of a common variation of the traditional ordering system. This lies in its use of multiple stationery for ordering. Orders are typed on a 5in × 3in four-part set. These sets come in perforated strips (each strip comprising five sets) so that they can be readily wound through a typewriter. The top two copies of the four-part set go to the bookseller, who returns the second of these with the book or uses it as a report form. The third copy is filed numerically (each set is numbered) to constitute an 'on order' file. The fourth copy is filed in the library's author catalogue, and is removed when the permanent catalogue card for the book is filed.

The foregoing paragraphs present a number of examples of variations of traditional ordering methods, but none match in prospects for the future the type of computerized system which is now in operation at Newcastle. Previously Newcastle used edge-punched cards, but the system became (as it has done elsewhere) less and less satisfactory as the order file grew in size: the reason being that needle-sorting causes too much upheaval to be applied frequently to a large file. Newcastle*

* I am indebted to Mr R W Fern for these details.

now codes its orders with country, fund and bookseller codes, and punches them on to paper tape. This is then read into a computer, which stores the information on magnetic tape and prints it out, with comments, indicating where wrong codes have been used or where a punching-error has made an entry incomprehensible. Key punchers punch a correction tape from the printout, incorporating in it spelling corrections also, and run this into the computer. The computer corrects the original information and adds it to the master-file, on another magnetic tape. Parallel with this operation is the weekly input of corrections and alterations to the master-file itself. Each week a new master-file is produced, with the new orders on it, and with existing items marked up to show receipt or bookseller's report. At any given time the master-file will contain all items currently on order, and all items received since the previous August 1st.

Items being ordered are listed once a week, grouped by the computer into bookseller order. The computer expands the code for each bookseller to full name and address, and prints out the order four to a page, heading each page ' Newcastle upon Tyne University Library '. To provide an accessions register the computer produces weekly a list of items received, in accession-number order. The computer also produces reminder lists, selecting the outstanding orders from the file automatically; lists for academic departments, showing the items received by the library against each department's fund and those still on order; monthly lists of expenditure and commitments, sorted by fund; lists of items on order, sorted by bookseller; and other less-frequently needed lists—for example, of out-of-print books. The ability of this system to store ordering information, and to reconstitute such information in a multiplicity of ways, obviously goes far beyond that of any other described in this section.

PERIODICALS RECORDING

Since the ' average ' university library subscribes to about 3,000 periodical titles, and since most of these appear in weekly, monthly or quarterly parts, it will be apparent that the recording and checking procedures involved in their control are detailed and complex. Mention was made earlier in this chapter of the computerized periodicals checking-in system being developed at the City University: but this is very experimental. The standard, almost universal, system is the visible index system illustrated in plate 1. An entry for each periodical title is made on ruled cards, and these cards are housed in flat trays in an overlapping fashion so that all that is immediately visible in the opened tray is the edge of each card, which bears the name of the periodical. This makes each title easy to spot; the card is then flipped back by the periodicals assistant, and on it is recorded the arrival of each part. The cards are variously ruled by year into weeks, months or quarters so that the record of arrival is readily made; other spaces are provided for details such as source, location, date of original order, cost and so on.

Numerous other factors, however, complicate the whole conduct of periodicals recording. Changes are forever occurring: changes of title, of publishing body, of size, or periodicity, of price. The periodicals department has to keep a check on when a volume is complete; whether the title-page and index have been received; and whether there have been special supplements or issues. A great deal of correspondence is required in chasing up or replacing (sometimes by a photocopy from another library) missing parts. On top of this is the business of maintaining an accounting check on the payment of subscriptions. Most libraries prefer to use an agent through whom they can place their orders; if the agent is a good one, the library is spared a vast amount of tedious negotiation.

An adjunct to most periodicals departments is the ordering and recording of government and official publications. This is a major operation, and one which requires for its successful execution specialized knowledge and considerable expertise. Indeed, this is a branch of librarianship in its own right.

CATALOGUING

From the order department, a book proceeds to the cataloguing department. In most libraries still, the cataloguing department both catalogues and classifies books: though where there is a system of subject specialization (as described in chapter VI), it will certainly be the team of subject specialists who look after classification. To catalogue a book is to make a record of its bibliographical details—author, title, edition, collation, series, place of publication, publisher and date.

To classify a book is to diagnose what its subject is and assign it to a place in the classification system which the library uses; such subject classification can also involve choosing an appropriate subject heading for a subject catalogue.

A cataloguing department can be organized in a number of ways, the extent and variety of these ways being largely dependent on the size of the department's staff. A common form of organization, even in a library without a fully developed system of subject specialization, is in fact by subject: one cataloguer-classifier concentrating on scientific works, another literature, and so on. An equally common division is by language, since a high proportion of every university library's purchases are in a foreign language, and plainly a good knowledge of Russian or German or other language is required to catalogue books in those languages. Another way is to divide the work, to some extent, by type of material: one cataloguer being concerned, for example, with all ' continuations '—that is, further volumes or parts of sets or series which the library already possesses. Yet another way is to organize the work by process: in a two-man department, for example, one cataloguer might be responsible for the actual cataloguing, and the other for classification. Most departments employ a mixture of all of these to make the best use of whatever skills or special knowledge are available in the team.

Cataloguing practices and procedures have been recently surveyed by Friedman and Jeffreys in their report *Cataloguing and classification in British university libraries,* which was based on elaborate questionnaires completed by fifty one university and college libraries. Their first major finding is the predictable one that the majority of libraries (forty of the fifty one) favour a card catalogue; a lesser number use a sheaf catalogue (that is, catalogue slips in small loose-leaf binders); and a handful use a guard-book form of catalogue (that is, a series of large loose-leaf volumes into which entries are pasted on slips). At this point it is worth making some comments on these three physical forms of catalogue. The card catalogue is by far the easiest to administer: it is completely flexible, since cards can be filed and unfiled without difficulty. Cards are easy to produce and reproduce; they can also be provided in printed form by either the Library of Congress or the British National Bibliography. The disadvantages of the card catalogue are that it is extremely bulky; and worse still, that it is not easy to use. The guard-book form of catalogue is very troublesome and difficult to maintain, and most of those that still exist have all but broken down; but, on the other hand, it is impressively economical of space. The sheaf form of catalogue is an attempt to combine the flexibility of the card catalogue with the economy of space and ease of use of a book-form catalogue; but like most compromises it does not fully succeed in any of these respects.

Friedman and Jeffreys deal also with the filing rules used by university libraries for their catalogues. A library's main catalogue is always its author catalogue, and filing entries into this has to be done according to some consistent system. To misfile an entry is equivalent to losing a book, for if a reader cannot find a particular book recorded in the catalogue he must assume that the library does not possess it. The variety and complexity of the types of heading needed in an author catalogue demand a detailed code of filing rules: authors' surnames can be compounded of two words, or have a prefix; with some writers entry is made under forename; there are noblemen's titles to contend with; and, of course, some works are anonymous or pseudonymous. Apart from the difficulties which attach to entering under personal names, further difficulties arise from the fact that an ' author ' catalogue must contain entries under other kinds of names: institutions, societies, firms, and so on. Friedman and Jeffreys report that the filing code most used by university libraries in this country is the American Library Association's *Rules for filing catalog cards* (1942); others use the Library of Congress's *Filing rules in the dictionary catalogs* (1956), or Charles A Cutter's *Rules for a dictionary catalog* (fourth edition 1904), or the British Museum's *Guide to the arrangement of headings and entries in the General Catalogue of Printed Books;* and some have devised codes of their own.

Few books require only one entry in a library's author catalogue. Many books, for example, have two authors, and entry needs to be made under both: the basic entry (which is made under the name of the author mentioned first on the title-page) is known as the ' main ' entry, the other (under the name of the second author) as the ' added ' entry. Added entries can be abbreviated versions of the main entry, or even just references to it; however, Friedman and Jeffreys reveal

94

that in the majority of libraries the added entry used is a full version of the main entry—that is, it is an identical copy but with the extra heading added. Such entries are known as ' unit entries ', since the basic format never alters. This system is one very much to be preferred, since no matter what heading the reader chooses to look under, he will be supplied with full information and will need therefore to look no further. It is a kind of courtesy to help readers immediately in this way; there are few more dispiriting things than consulting a catalogue which obliges the user to pursue a perpetual chain of references, including a few blind-alleys for good measure. The unit entry system has also a supreme practical value; any form of added entry which is a departure from the basic record will involve a rewriting or retyping, whereas the unit system means that the basic version needs only straightforward duplication. In this context, Friedman and Jeffreys report that about half of the libraries surveyed by them are therefore able to use duplicating or offset-litho machines, or xerox machines, or tape-typewriters, to manufacture automatically the sets of cards they need.

Cataloguing productivity is a major concern to all libraries. The operation is always an expensive one, and a close check must be kept on output. It is standard practice for a cataloguing department to report its annual overall statistic; but more frequent, and more individual, statistics should be demanded. Without fail, this type of demand seems to produce better output: a cataloguer who is obliged to offer a daily account (which need mean no more than writing on a slip the number of books he has catalogued that day) of his work tends to approach his task and apportion his time in a more rigorous and realistic way than he might do otherwise. Cataloguing is the kind of occupation in which it is very easy to become self-indulgent.

One difficulty which Friedman and Jeffreys encountered was in trying to establish the productivity rate of an ' average ' cataloguer per year: the figure varied enormously—for example, one library claimed 7,000 titles per cataloguer per year, whereas another library of exactly the same type claimed only 1,000 titles per cataloguer per year. The likeliest average figure seems to be about 3,000 titles per year. Friedman and Jeffreys note that this coincides with the figure recommended in the *Guide to Canadian university library standards: report of the University Library Standards Committee of the Canadian*

Association of College and University Libraries, 1961-1964 (1965). From this same Canadian report, Friedman and Jeffreys select a number of other cataloguing standards which seem acceptable: these include the statement that a competent cataloguer should be able to work after one year without anyone needing to revise what he has done; and that normally a book should be catalogued within one month of its arrival in the cataloguing department, and should certainly never remain there longer than three months.

Friedman and Jeffreys also found difficulty in establishing the factors which affect productivity. All that they can really say is that libraries which invariably tried to establish the full Christian names of authors were among those with the lowest output figures; as were those libraries whose cataloguers wrote out rather than typed the original cataloguing copy. Even this last is open to question, and is flatly contradicted by Woledge and Page who write that ' experience shows that, in a library of any size, it is an economy . . . to write slips, from which typists can make the entries: a cataloguer must be a highly skilled person, and it is a waste of his salary to employ him on the relatively unskilled work of the typist '.

Friedman and Jeffreys were not able to discover any relation between output and the cataloguing code used. If it is true that filing must be done according to an agreed and consistent system, it is equally true that actual cataloguing must be conducted likewise. The most popular code in British university libraries (being used by over half of them) is the Anglo-American Joint Code (1908); next in popularity (being used by a third of the libraries surveyed) is the ALA (the American Library Association) code (second edition 1949). No doubt both of these will be displaced by the new *Anglo-American cataloguing rules*, published in 1967.

All that has been said so far in this section has concerned the author catalogue (which is in fact in the majority of libraries a ' name ' catalogue—that is, as well as the names of those who wrote books it also contains the names of those who are the subjects of books), but also important in a library is its subject catalogue. Over three-quarters of the libraries surveyed by Friedman and Jeffreys provide some kind of subject catalogue, and what they mostly provide is a classified catalogue—that is, the arrangement of the entries following precisely that of the classification scheme used by the library. Such a catalogue needs an alphabetical index to it. However, by far and away the best type of catalogue is the alphabetical-subject catalogue, in which the entry for each book is given a subject heading, and then filed alphabetically by this heading. Why this is the superior form of subject catalogue is that, first of all, it is the most popular with the library's users (especially with undergraduates), and secondly because it gives a subject approach to the library which is independent of (and probably infinitely preferable to) that provided by the shelf classification. A classified catalogue, on the other hand, though it is more convenient administratively for the library staff, can do little more than mimic the library's shelf arrangement, and is notoriously confusing and unhelpful as far as the library's users are concerned. A great deal of nonsense has been written to the effect that a classified catalogue is altogether a finer-edged bibliographical tool; maybe it is, but since so few readers use it, it is entirely self-defeating.

One of the things which the Friedman and Jeffreys report confirms completely is the fact that few British university libraries make use of existing centralized cataloguing services. The reasons for this are not reprehensible, nor just to do with local pride or idiosyncratic attitudes. Of the two available printed catalogue card services currently available—the British National Bibliography's service and that of the Library of Congress—the first covers less than 40 percent of the ' average ' British university library's intake, and the second is far too dilatory for subscribers in this country. It is nevertheless a disturbing thought that at any one period, up and down the country, the same title is being catalogued independently and expensively by some fifty or sixty university libraries. D J Foskett, in his article *The intellectual and social challenge of the library service*, criticizes this situation not merely in library terms, but in human terms also, as a 'waste of people's lives '. R E Ellsworth, in his Cornell Library Conference paper, is equally insistent that cataloguing must be centralized, because until this is the case ' each university library will be saddled with cataloguing costs that are unforgivably high '.

As was noted in an earlier section of this chapter, centralized cataloguing has come at the present time to mean almost exclusively the Library of Congress's MARC project, linked in this country with the

97

BNB. MARC is an acronym (MAchine-Readable Cataloguing) for the Library of Congress project to supply centrally cataloguing data for current books in the form of magnetic tape which individual libraries can then use, through the medium of a computer, to produce their own catalogue entries. Though the data for each book is offered in a very full form, each individual library will be able to select only what it considers relevant for its own catalogue. MARC's coverage is very wide: it will supply cataloguing data for all books, no matter where published, required by university and research libraries. To achieve this MARC is co-operating with national cataloguing agencies, and therefore there is now in existence an international network supplying cataloguing data to the Library of Congress. It is only by means of such a system that libraries will be able to control bibliographically the 450,000-500,000 titles published annually in the world today. A great deal of investigation is now being conducted in this country on the actual use and application of MARC tapes, and this will necessarily take some time: but tackling the cataloguing problem on this kind of international scale makes very much more sense than (in the words of A J Wells in his article *Shared cataloguing: a new look at an old problem*) ' the losing battle we fight in trying to create and maintain our individual catalogues '.

A recent development linked with computerized cataloguing is COM (computer output on to Microfilm). One of the problems of computer-generated catalogues is the expense of reproducing them for the library's users. The City of Westminster adopted a computerized cataloguing system in the late 1960's, employing a straight author listing. Since the Westminster libraries needed 25 copies of their catalogue, photocopying was used to produce that number. Offset-litho printing was considered, but it would have caused too much delay. However, photocopying also proved to be too slow, and very expensive into the bargain. As a result, the City of Westminster adopted the COM system, whereby computer-held data is transferred directly on to mircofilm. Public catalogues are therefore in the form of 16 mm film cassettes, and are consulted on hand-operated readers (see plate 9). Diazo film, which is virtually indestructible, is used; and a negative image is preferred. The system has been fully operational since April 1971, and public reaction is good.

The Westminster system was examined in detail by Birmingham University Library; and now the pre-1972 catalogue there has been converted to microfilm and made available in 35 copies scattered throughout the campus and the library itself. From April 1973 COM will be used by Birmingham as the output medium for the new mechanized MARC-based catalogue which will cover all the library's serials and all monographs acquired after 1st January 1972.

Apart from being cheap, fast and effective, the COM system is very economical of space. Whereas the catalogue of Westminster would take up 50 cubic feet in card form, or 5 cubic feet in bound books (20 volumes), one copy of the microfilm with microfilm reader takes up only 4 cubic feet. It is therefore to be expected that the use of COM will spread to other university libraries besides Birmingham.

Even COM, of course, is only a stage, until library users can interrogate library computers directly.

CLASSIFICATION
The Friedman and Jeffreys report notes that of the fifty one university libraries surveyed, twenty five use the Library of Congress Classification, twenty two the Dewey Decimal Classification, seventeen the Universal Decimal Classification, and five the Bliss Classification. There are other schemes used—some libraries have their own, but the four mentioned are the major ones.

The Library of Congress scheme is the most common because it is the most appropriate: its schedules are full and scholarly and their general arrangement is nearest to academic needs. However, this statement must be regarded as a very relative one: none of the general schemes is really satisfactory or intellectually acceptable, and the Library of Congress scheme has the added disadvantage of dating from the beginning of this century. Dewey, the next most popular, has the advantages of a basically simple structure and a more easily remembered and more readily apprehended notation; but its general approach is more suited to a public than to an academic library, and in addition, it dates from even further back—from 1876. The Universal Decimal Classification finds most favour in libraries with a strong technological bias—Friedman and Jeffreys observe that of the seventeen universities using it, eight were formerly colleges of advanced technology. The remaining major general scheme, the Bliss Classification, has a brief notation and a careful arrangement of major classes; but being a one-man scheme which came rather late on the established scene it has missed being widely adopted.

Book classification in Britain has been given almost too much attention. While it can be readily acknowledged that none of the major general schemes is satisfactory, and that extensive areas of each are woefully inadequate, it has also to be recognized that no large library can do very much to improve matters. It would be possible to set up a massive reclassification programme, but the library concerned would have to be very sure of the merits of the scheme it proposed to substitute for its old one: and the truth of the matter is that there does not exist any scheme of that degree of merit; indeed, if there were, the passage of only a few years (and university libraries operate on a very long time-scale) and the attendant growth of knowledge would reduce aspects and areas of it to inadequacy also. This is not so defeatist as it sounds. The position is that if a library uses one of the standard schemes mentioned most of the essential purposes of a classification scheme are served. The books are arranged in a recognizable order, by subject; that order is signalled by class-marks; those class-marks act as the link between the catalogue and the shelves. The main tool in a university library is the author catalogue; the classification scheme is only an ancillary help. Users of an academic library do browse around the shelves, and do go to main subject areas; but for detailed searching they must rely on catalogues and bibliographies.

This section so far has been concerned mostly with what might be called the public aspect of book classification in a university library. But there is an internal aspect also. A great deal of vigilance and discretion must be observed in the matter of applying any classification scheme. It was stressed earlier how most schemes are without intrinsic merit, invariably out-of-date, and in many areas grossly inadequate. Therefore if a classifier spends hours applying to books the most elaborate and complicated Library of Congress table or the ultimate Dewey decimal point, it can only be regarded as an extremely wasteful exercise. I have challenged the practice of such close classification in my article *Book classification in new university libraries*; and there, as here, advocate the adoption of broader, simpler classification (though rigorously and consistently applied). The necessary corollary to this is the provision of an efficient alphabetical-subject catalogue. Views similar to these have since been expressed also by M B Line and P Bryant in their article *How golden is your retriever?*

Woledge and Page note the two factors which must be borne in mind when choosing or applying a classification system in an academic library: ' First, that a university public is critical of the arbitrary and irrational, and inclined to be impatient of class-marks elaborated beyond apparent reason. And secondly, that though it is unnecessary to follow exactly the divisions of the academic curriculum, it is inconvenient to cut across them too much.' In brief, classify according to use, and classify broadly.

BINDING AND PREPARATION

When a book has been catalogued and classified, it must then be made ready for the shelves. Since a large proportion of any university library's intake is of foreign or old material, this very often involves the binding of items. This is one of the reasons why ' binding ' features so importantly in its budget (see the section on finance in chapter I); the other main reasons are firstly, the vast amount of binding which is necessitated by the large numbers of periodicals taken and retained by a university library, and secondly, the constant need for repair and maintenance of books (since university libraries discard very little of their stock).

Most libraries still send items which require binding to commercial binderies, but an increasing number are setting up their own binderies. The Woledge and Page statement on this—' Long experience and careful investigation indicate that only the very largest institution can profitably have its own bindery, but persons whose service is to " stand and wait " may usefully be trained in the art of repairing books with simple materials '— no longer holds true. First of all, library budgets have increased tremendously since Woledge and Page wrote their *Manual,* and the volume of intake in all medium-sized institutions would justify the setting-up of a bindery. Secondly, there are very few persons in a university library nowadays who would fall into any 'stand

and wait' category; nor would many librarians entrust to such even the simplest forms of book repair: this type of amateurism has fallen into a deserved disrepute. Gelfand in his *University libraries for developing countries* offers an equally unsatisfactory criterion: 'In general, when the volume of binding work is large enough so that it is cheaper for the library to do its own than to send it out, establishment of a library binding department should be considered.' In fact, to justify a library bindery on the grounds that it does the work more cheaply than a commercial firm is not necessary. All that must be shown is that it costs no more, because the real gains for a library in having a bindery of its own are not mainly financial ones.

The first of these gains is that the library staff are able to deal with binding matters on a closer and more direct basis; since the bindery is under their own roof, they can give much more specific instructions and easily check that such instructions are carried out. To be able to negotiate matters of detail and special treatment on a continuous basis is extremely valuable. By the same token, it is easier to arrange priorities for the work which has to be done. It is also a great advantage that library materials never leave the premises: any item can always be retrieved if necessary. A further gain is that a library bindery is usually able to maintain a higher standard of work than can be obtained from a commercial firm, since the control of this is in the library's own hands. Yet another is that a library bindery can accommodate a great deal of purely repair work, as opposed to complete binding. In older libraries, such repair and maintenance of stock is a massive problem. It is very expensive to have such work done by a commercial firm, since it cannot be done on a factory basis by them and each item has to receive individual (and therefore costlier) treatment. A library bindery is also able to do a variety of jobs not strictly connected with bookbinding: making special pamphlet boxes and cases, mounting signs and photographs for library exhibitions, and so on. Finally, the university generally appreciates the availability of a bindery on the campus; the library binders are usually able to undertake private work for university staff, and to bind theses for students.

One of the best examples in Britain of a bindery in a medium-sized library is that at the University of Reading. This bindery (see plate 2) employs a chief binder, four journeyman binders, an apprentice binder and five part-time sewers. The annual cost (1973) of running it is as follows:

Staff:

Chief binder	£2,750
4 binders (£1,365 + 8 hours overtime weekly = £1,815)	7,260
Apprentice	£1,030
5 part-time sewers (145 hours weekly at 48p per hour)	£3,620
Materials	£1,600
	£16,260

The usual annual output is 7,000 volumes bound, and 4,000 minor repairs. Obviously this does not include overheads such as heating and lighting; nor does it take account of the capital cost of the equipment used, which is as follows.

Guillotine 32″	£1,500
Board cutter	£300
Small board and paper cutter	£35
Backing machine	£425
4 nipping presses	£450
Glueing machine and stand	£125
4 glue pots (electric)	£80
Blocking press—series 1	£200
Finishing tools and type	£500
Laminating press	£100
	£3,715

These costs (an initial equipping sum of approximately £3,715 and an annual recurrent sum of approximately £16,260) are modest in view of the advantages arising from a library having its own bindery. There must, however, as always, be one major cautionary note. To take on the administration of a library bindery has all the risks which attach to any piece of administration: it involves careful planning, satisfactory staffing and firm control. If a library bindery works well, fine; if it does not, then it is a nightmare. The importance of binding work in a university library is such that it must not be mishandled as an operation. It would be far better to use one of the commercial firms (which in this country are on the whole very reliable) than be saddled with an inefficient bindery. The secret, as in all key departments in a library, is to choose the chief operative very carefully indeed. Mismanagement invariably manifests itself in the form of poor productivity: and serious hold-ups in binding effectively cripple the work of a library.

Books which do not require binding, still need to undergo various kinds of preparation before they are placed on the shelves. First they must have possession marks added to them—stamped with the name of the library and/or have the library's book-plate affixed to them. The other important task is marking as permanently as possible the spine of the book with its class-mark—this can be done with a stylus, or with various forms of label or tape. The ' preparations ' department is also usually responsible for making minor repairs, and is the department which processes items in readiness for binding.

STOCKTAKING

Even after a book has been placed on the shelves of the library it is important to make periodic checks on its existence and to see that it and its records continue to match. An annual stocktaking is not the universal practice it once was, but there is much to be said for it. First of all, ' stocktaking ' is something of a misnomer: the main purpose is not in fact to discover which books are missing. This aspect is important, but it is really only incidental. A better name for the operation is ' inspection ': that is, once a year a library puts its house in order, making sure that its books are all traceable and all in order, and that its various records and catalogues are accurate. All sorts of errors creep into a library system, and such an inspection constitutes an essential ' spring clean ' after one academic session and in readiness for the next.

The actual mechanics of an annual inspection are very straightforward. The basic record used is the shelf-register—ordinarily in the form of cards which are arranged precisely in the order in which the library's books are shelved. The library staff is divided into teams of two, each team being assigned to a particular area of the shelves. One of the team ' reads ' the shelves (that is, calls out the author, title and class-mark of each book) and the other member checks off the shelf-register cards accordingly. Cards for which there are no books are put to one side; similarly, books for which there are no cards; and similarly cases where book and card do not properly match. A necessary preliminary to stocktaking, or inspection, is the recall of all library books from users; a necessary follow-up are the weeks of work (usually by the cataloguing department) required to clear up queries of all sorts and to make such amendments as are called for to books and records. To see the volume of such queries in even a well-run library is sufficient proof in itself of the need for a regular (not necessarily annual, and not necessarily the whole collection at one time) check.

VI

READER SERVICES

BORROWING FACILITIES: University libraries, with a few notable exceptions—such as the Bodleian—are lending libraries. The greater part of a university library's stock is freely available to readers. Only certain categories of material are restricted to use within the library. Reference books, standard bibliographies and printed catalogues, and abstracts and indexes cannot, obviously, be borrowed. Nor are rare and valuable items from special collections (as described in chapter IV) normally allowed to leave the library premises. If a library runs an undergraduate collection in the form of a reserve book collection (as described in chapter IV also), again the general rule does not apply. Also, because of the heavy use made of them, periodical volumes and parts (especially the latter) are usually subject to some degree of restriction.

However, all users of an academic library do not enjoy identical borrowing privileges. These differ according to the status of the user, of which there are three main categories: undergraduates, postgraduates, and academic staff. Borrowing privileges mirror this ascending order precisely. A typical pattern would be that undergraduates can borrow up to six volumes for two weeks, postgraduates twelve volumes for two months, and academic staff twenty volumes for an unlimited period. Of course, such a basic pattern is capable of endless variation, both in the number of volumes allowed and in the period of loan, but the essential distinction between the categories is everywhere observed. There are other categories, too—non-academic staff, BEd students, and so on—and the borrowing privileges accorded to each of these is a matter decided upon by the library committee, though with a certain amount of discretionary power being left in the hands of the university librarian. All university libraries receive many visitors from outside their own academic community, but while they are invariably willing to grant reference or consultation facilities, they as a general rule do not allow such visitors to borrow books. Under this heading come students on vacation from other universities: they are welcome, indeed encouraged, to read in the library, but not to borrow books from it.

Two main problems arise from the granting of borrowing privileges, both to do with maintaining the availability of books. If a book which is wanted by one reader is out on loan to another, it is necessary to operate an effective recall and reservation service. This is simply a matter of sending a postcard to the first reader advising him that somebody else is waiting to use the book currently in his possession, and of marking the issue record (that is, the record of books on loan) in such a way that when the book is returned it is put to one side and the person who requested it informed. The second problem is retrieving overdue books from forgetful, or selfish, readers. Most university libraries charge fines as a deterrent, but there are many reasons why this is not a satisfactory method. For one thing, it is expensive, especially of staff time: it is, as the Americans say, spending dimes to collect nickels. Secondly, if the fines mount up too quickly on a book, it is self-defeating, because the fact that there are such fines to pay becomes a further reason for not returning the book. Thirdly, fines create an atmosphere of antagonism out of all proportion to their doubtful success in ensuring the prompt return of books; the library begins to look to uninformed minds like a money-grabbing organization: there are still library readers who believe that libraries are built, stocked and staffed out of money obtained from fines. Fourthly, it should always be remembered that the readers who abuse their borrowing privileges are in the minority, and it is a bad policy to gear the whole system to accommodate them rather than to suit those who by and large conduct themselves responsibly. And fifthly, since a library's users are not in any way financially uniform, a fines system cannot work equitably.

It is far better to rely on persuasion for the return of overdue books. Two or three reminders bring most books back; if these have no result, it is usually effective to inform students (who constitute the largest element in a university library's readership and therefore tend to feature most prominently in its overdues transactions) that the next step will be to contact their tutors. The final step, to deal with the

107

absolutely recalcitrant, is to send a bill for the replacement value of the book or books, payment of such a bill often being enforceable by the university authorities. However, this ultimate procedure is required for only a tiny percentage of offenders, and it is a fair guess that this same tiny percentage would be just as intractable—maybe even more so—if a system of punitive fines were in operation. The absence of a fines system helps to create an atmosphere of trust and co-operation.

The stock of even the largest of university libraries is not sufficient to meet all the demands of all its users. Scholars and researchers frequently need to consult works which are only available in other libraries. Consequently, a university library needs to participate in the national and international network of inter-library loans. This aspect of borrowing facilities is dealt with more fully in chapter VIII, which is concerned with co-operation between libraries.

ISSUE SYSTEMS

It will be appreciated from the foregoing account of borrowing facilities in a university library that the accurate recording of loans is very important. It is also important that the loans record—usually called the issue, or circulation, system—should readily provide the answers to a number of questions: who has this book? which books does this reader have? how long has this reader had this book?

The commonest, and cheapest, issue system in university libraries is that based on a two-part slip. The reader fills in a slip for each book which he wishes to borrow. The slip is headed with the name of the library, and the main details required are: the author's name; the title, class-mark and accession number of the book; the reader's name and his signature; and the date. The reader then hands the book and the slip to the assistant at the library exit counter. The assistant stamps the book's date label, and the slip, with the date when the book is due for return; gives the reader the book; and retains the slip. Subsequently the slip (the second part of which is self-carboning; or else there is a piece of carbon-paper interleaved) is separated into its two parts, one of which is filed alphabetically into an author file, the other into a borrower's file by date. From the first of these two files can be answered the question: who has this book? From the second file can be answered the questions: which books does this reader have? how long has this reader had this book? The defects of the system are first, it is something of an imposition on readers to require them to spend so much time filling in issue slips; second, because the slips are filled in by hand, and usually at some speed, and because the reader does not always find it easy to identify accurately the book's details, it is all too usual for such slips to be imperfect records; third, it is a time-consuming exercise to divide and file the slips, and subsequently unfile them; and fourth, the resultant record, composed of flimsy pieces of paper a high percentage of which are inaccurate or illegible, is clumsy and inefficient to use.

Attempts to simplify and reduce this bulky record have been a predictable development. The first line of attack was to try to reduce the number of slips needed, and to make do with one sequence rather than two; however, it was obvious to many librarians that a radically different approach was required. The library at the University of Sussex, for example, when first established, adopted a system based on the use of punched cards. The issue system was maintained on ' dual-purpose ' punched cards, the right-hand section of each card being completed by the borrower (date borrowed, borrower's number, book number, author and title of book, borrower's signature), and the left-hand section punched accordingly by a punch operator. These cards were mechanically sorted into a single file in book-number order; when a book was returned, the relevant card was withdrawn manually. A collator could extract mechanically cards representing books on loan to a particular borrower, or books which were due for return on a particular date. The obvious advantage of such a system was that it reduced the amount of manual filing and unfiling required. However, it still left the reader with the chore of filling in the issue record, which in its turn created the problem of inaccurate records—in this case, the whole efficiency of the system depended entirely on the borrower's accuracy in transcribing a six-figure book-number.

The library at the new University of York adopted the Bookamatic system, whereby each book in the library is provided with a plastic card embossed with author and title details, and each reader with a plastic ticket embossed with his name and address. To record an issue, all that is needed is for these two plastic cards to be placed in a hand-operated Addressograph machine which then prints off the record required. The advantages of the system are precisely those on which the Sussex system falls down; first, the reader has no filling in to do, and second, the records are always accurate and always legible. The major drawback is that such a system could only be readily introduced when, as was the case at York, the library was starting from scratch and the plastic cards could be made for the books as they were acquired. In an established library, the provision of such cards retrospectively would be a daunting task.

The real breakthrough in the design of issue systems has come with the application of computers to library routines, as described in the relevant section of chapter V. The pioneer here was the library at Southampton University. In common with many other British universities Southampton expanded rapidly in the period 1963-67, and this rapid growth imposed strains on the existing library clerical systems. Coincidentally the university was provided with a powerful third generation computer which, though it was intended mainly for scientific research, led to consideration of its use for the library. In 1966 a Data Processing Unit was established to give a supporting service to the library and the university administration, and this provided the necessary staff to design and prepare the computer system. A grant from the Office of Scientific and Technical Information subsequently permitted the appointment of a systems analyst and two programmers to develop automated library systems.

At Southampton, each reader has a card designed in laminated plastic with a paper insert punched with his number, and each book has a book-card punched with details of its author, title, class-mark and accession number. The issue of a book to a reader is made by feeding these cards through a data collection machine, which records the transaction on a paper tape. The paper tape is fed into the university computer, which produces a daily print-out. Cancelling a loan is similarly automatic, as are other routines such as the sending of overdue notices.

The Southampton system has been fully described by B A J McDowell and C M Phillips (Southampton University Library, *Automation Project Report No. 1*), who also outline its proposed future development to an on-line system.

A commercially-available issue system, developed by Automated

Library Systems Ltd (see Plate 3), is now in operation in the university libraries of Sussex, Surrey and East Anglia, and will soon be installed at Newcastle and Reading. The basic difference is that the book-card uses the accession-number only. At Surrey, it is also now planned to introduce an on-line system.

ACCESS TO BOOKS

In their *Manual*, which was published in 1940, Woledge and Page supply what amounts to an historical note on the matter of access by readers to the stock of a university library: ' Direct access to the shelves is the keynote of the sweeping change which came over library service to readers in the last generation. Books in certain categories, it is now almost universally held, must be directly accessible to those who need them, and the resources of library planning and administration are largely directed to this end. Formerly, books were requisitioned from a catalogue, and were delivered in a reading room, there to be read.' Statistical proof of this statement is supplied by Friedman and Jeffreys in their survey: of the fifty one libraries who returned questionnaires, forty four (eighty six percent) were entirely or mainly open, and only seven (fourteen percent) had closed access, and even that in all seven cases was partial not total.

Nobody now would contemplate refusing readers free access to most of a university library's books; the principle is completely accepted. But recently, the debate has been reopened, most notably by F W Ratcliffe in his article *Problems of open access in large academic libraries*. He harks back to some of the points Woledge and Page felt obliged to make; namely, in their words, that unrestricted access does create serious problems of ' seating accommodation, efficient control and correct replacement of books ', and of ensuring that the library is ' reasonably quiet and unobstructed ' so as to remain a possible place for study. But he adds many more telling arguments to these. Open access, for example, necessitates the expense and trouble of classification; a closed access system requires only accession order. Open access, again, is one of the major reasons why library buildings have to be larger and yet larger; closed access permits a much more economical shelving of books. The risks of theft, disarrangement and mutilation which open access creates force one, he says, to acknowledge the fact that if in the closed access libraries of mid-Europe and Scandinavia 'the way of the book is slower, it is more certain than in England'. He also queries the much-stressed 'educational value' of open access, pointing out that at least closed access made librarian/reader confrontation obligatory, and remarking: 'I sometimes feel that the tremendous demands for and necessity of instruction in library use is an absolute indictment of the open access principle'. Two other practical points he notes are that 'bibliographical skills are not encouraged by open access'—use of the catalogues, for example; and that an open access system makes it very difficult to obtain proper statistics of library use. Overall, the picture he paints is one of students wandering lost and confused, and researchers trying to rely on browsing.

Now Dr Ratcliffe is not really being reactionary, nor trying to put back the clock. Indeed, his own library at Manchester is proud of its open access history. His main arguments are three in number, and all of them valid. The first is that open access has been universally adopted without due regard to its inevitable implications. The second is that there must always be certain areas of the library—store collections, for example, or special collections—which cannot be readily accessible to every one of the library's readers. And the third is that the principle of entire open access becomes less defensible when the library is of a major order: 'There is an optimum size beyond which open stacks are a liability, a luxury and a decided disservice to readers to say nothing of staff'.

Proof of what Dr Ratcliffe says is offered in the next three sections of this book, which are concerned with the services which become necessary if the library operates on the open access principle: if, in fact, the library really accepts the implications of open access.

REFERENCE SERVICES

Gelfand acknowledges the implications of open access by carefully identifying the two main aspects of reader services. First, 'library materials should be highly accessible and easily available for use by all members of the university community'; but second, and this is accepting the implications of the first, 'assistance in the location of materials and in the use of the library for information and research should also be available '.

'Assistance in the location of materials ' is reference service at its simplest level, and is usually provided at the library's enquiry desk. Examples of such a service are: locating in the catalogue an item for which a reader has searched unsuccessfully, or confirming for him that in fact it is not in stock; showing a reader how to find from the subject catalogue what books the library has on a particular topic; taking a reader to the various printed indexes through which he can trace the particular periodical article he requires; and telling a reader which work of reference he should consult to discover a certain piece of information. This type of reference service also extends to producing the actual information required as opposed merely to indicating where it might be found: answers to telephone queries have to be of this nature.

However, when a reference enquiry is not of this ' quick reference ' type, but one where more time and effort is involved, then a second level of reference service must be provided. So far most libraries have only been able to offer the services of one person, usually called ' reference assistant ' or ' reader's adviser ' or (as at Reading) ' bibliographical consultant '. Examples of his or her tasks are: helping readers with difficult bibliographical references (that is, ones involving long and skilled searching); compiling reading-lists in collaboration with members of the teaching staff; compiling bibliographies; bringing to the notice of members of the teaching staff details of publications relevant to their work; and advising on information techniques. It is the hope in many libraries that the provision of this type of assistance to readers can be increased; some libraries, Southampton for example, have already managed to appoint a number of what are now most frequently described as ' information officers '.

SUBJECT SPECIALIZATION

Very relevant to the whole question of reference services is the concept of subject specialization, mentioned earlier in the context of staff structure, in Chapter III. A principal duty of a subject specialist is, of course, to offer an expert reference, information and bibliographical service in his particular field. In addition, he will bring his subject knowledge to bear on book selection duties, thereby making that process a more sure and informed one; likewise, in the cataloguing and classification of materials in his field, his subject expertise will protect him from errors caused by ignorance.

Subject specialization in its purest form has been practised in the University of East Anglia Library for ten years, from the very beginnings of that library. The university librarian, W L Guttsman, in his article *Subject specialization in academic libraries,* reiterates that his guiding principle was to ' amalgamate functions in the library and have subject specialists working in a field of knowledge but covering in respect of it book selection, classification, bibliography and reference work '. He describes the essential elements of his staff organization thus: 'Appointments in the Assistant Librarian grade and above are made for subject specializations in one or more specific fields and they seek to attract people with a relevant academic background. All members of the senior library staff act as subject specialists and are responsible, wholly or partially, for book selection in their field of specialization, or for the appropriate co-ordination of acquisitions where, as in the sciences, this is primarily done by faculty. Subject specialists will also deal with specialist bibliographical enquiries and give instruction to undergraduate or graduate students in bibliographical or information retrieval aspects of the subject whenever we can gain the support of the Schools and others concerned. They also classify, but do not catalogue, all books in their subjects and assign subject entries to them. In addition, they share a range of administrative tasks, but this is often more by way of consultative advice and general oversight of certain areas of library activity than by extensive part-time involvement. Conversely, certain areas of library services, eg, the issue desk, ordering department and periodical accessions are under the day-to-day control of senior library assistants, who control the activities of the junior staff assigned to these departments.'

He notes that since library salaries form only 40 percent of his total library expenditure, compared with the more usual figure of 50 percent found in British universities, the system can hardly be regarded as wasteful in terms of staff. However, he also adds that the system probably best fits universities with a student population of between 3,000-8,000 and with a fairly unified library system.

In Guttsman's view, subject specialization is justified in terms of service to readers, and in the building up of book collections. The greatest conflict, he says, arises 'between subject specialization and the maximization of efficiency'. Instead of a hierarchical structure of functional departments operating in an almost military fashion, 'decision-making becomes more diffused, and probably prolonged' since all senior subject specialists are involved in the process, under the chairmanship (rather than the management) of the university librarian. Moreover, another potential pitfall is that having left the 'old-fashioned library autocracy' behind, there is a tendency to create 'a variety of individual library systems' which can become mutually less compatible as time goes on and can even run counter to the uniformity and integration which is in the best interests of all users.

Another version of subject specialization is that (as at York University Library) whereby the basic organization is traditional in that there are identifiable Acquisitions, Cataloguing and Reader Services Departments, but superimposed on this is a scheme of subject responsibility. Staff do most of the cataloguing and classification within their own field. An even weaker version of this is the system which once operated in some university libraries whereby each member of the library staff, in addition to being responsible for some technical function in the library (binding preparation, cataloguing, book ordering or whatever), was also supposed to maintain an interest in a particular section of the library's shelves. The difficulty about this kind of subject specialization is that in a functionally-arranged library, functions must come first, and any kind of subject responsibility not only comes a very poor second at best but is also likely to be forgone completely in times of stress and pressure.

The commonest system of subject specialization is the creation of subject divisions within a library. There are many British examples of this. One of the first was at Glasgow University Library, where the new library building is in effect a series of subject libraries: Biological Sciences, Physical Sciences, Social Sciences and Humanities. Each of these divisions is staffed by a relevant team of specialists who between them can supply most of the subject expertise required of that division. At Southampton University Library a similar system of divisional libraries obtains, with an Assistant Librarian, who looks after both book selection and classification, in charge of each. The University of London Library has also created a string of 'subject libraries'—Music Library, United States Library, Latin American Library, Geography/Geology/Map Library, Philosophy Library, Psychology Library and History Library—and is well pleased with the arrangement; readers seem to find it a great convenience, and, claims the university librarian, the system makes the development of balanced collections a more straightforward operation. Surrey University Library's new building (1972) is another example, being divided, as its *Guide to the library* shows, into a Science and Engineering Area, a Social Sciences Area, a Languages and Literature Area and a History Area. However, the same *Guide* points out that 'every course within the university is inter-disciplinary with others, and that relevant material will inevitably be found at a number of places in the library '.

In defence of subject divisional arrangements, it should be remembered that for most users, libraries are large, entirely confusing places. If they realize that one area of the library is devoted to their field of interest, and if they find there a librarian who is knowledgeable in that field, then their relations with the library develop very much more vigorously. What is more, it is for them a very convenient arrangement that this same librarian not only assists them in a reference and bibliographical way, but is also the channel for recommendations for book purchase, and the classifier who can be approached about the actual arrangement of the books on the shelves. This is all the more attractive when one considers the alternative offered to the user by a library organized according to function: a deserted (and probably poorly guided) section of the shelves; an enquiry desk at a considerable distance from those shelves; and an Acquisitions Department and a Cataloguing Department both staffed by strangers apparently unacquainted with the user's field of interest.

However, the subject divisional system also has its critics. Ralph Ellsworth (in Brown: *Planning the academic library*) has recounted his experience as follows: 'I should like to make a brief evaluation of the subject divisional plan and I can do so objectively because I

116

had to abolish the system at Colorado—it didn't work. The good thing about it was first, it did bring books and students together in a manner helpful to the students. Second, the idea of having a subject divisional expert was a good one—that part worked. Those two advantages were balanced by the following disadvantages. It began to be clear that the terms were artificial. In a fixed-function building with separate rooms for the humanities and for the social sciences, quarrels began immediately. We had a Philosophy professor at that time who was very much interested in Marxism and economics. He insisted that the economics books be brought over to the humanities, and the history faculty began to object. Some of them thought of themselves as humanists, some of them thought of themselves as social scientists, and the young weak-minded librarian was caught between these philosophical forces. It is becoming increasingly difficult to put a label on subject blocks that means very much, to draw a distinction between some of the sciences and some of the social sciences, or between the social sciences and the humanities.

'The second difficulty was that the divisional reference experts were separated from the card catalogue and we couldn't afford to duplicate this catalogue. We could have a shop list in each room, but we couldn't put in a full subject catalogue. To us this is a very serious matter, because much reference work is done from the subject catalogue as well as from the author catalogue. The divisional librarians would always be running down to the central reference room, and the duplication of national bibliographies and other reference tools would be very expensive and a real problem. Then of course, in a fixed-function building, the plan broke down immediately because it was never possible to predict in advance how fast the collections would grow, nor to practise " bibliothecal birth control " on them, because the faculty would not stand for that, so you were caught with the fact that the student book ratio in the humanities was much lower than it was in the social sciences and the rooms immediately got out of balance. Nebraska has kept on with the divisional plan, but it was abandoned in Colorado eight or nine years ago because I could see it would not work '.

In our own country, Leicester University Library abandoned its subject divisional arrangement for much the same reasons. The university librarian felt that it was too cumbersome for a smooth and reasonably efficient co-ordination of work, and was dissatisfied with the incoherence, disunity and confusion which he believes results from a library operating on a subject-divided basis.

In conclusion though, two points must be made. First, it has been demonstrated by all libraries which have adopted some form of subject specialization, that no library can be operated successfully on a strictly functional basis. A library by its very nature must be client-oriented. Both Colorado and Leicester, while abandoning subject divisions, have retained an extensive reference service. The second point is that it is obviously wrong—as used to be the case—to concentrate all the staff of a library in one area and leave the rest of the building unmanned. The University of Hull has solved this problem in quite a simple way, without resorting to any subject divisional arrangement. The university librarian has appointed a number of ' floor managers ' who supervise shelving on a floor, keep an inconspicuous watch on the discipline of both readers and junior staff, fill in spare moments with stocktaking and minor repairs, answer readers' enquiries or refer them to the appropriate senior staff, and generally see to the smooth running of the floors.

GUIDES

A further implication of an open access library is that readers must be offered various kinds of guides to its use. This is an area in which many academic libraries have previously failed; having removed the barriers to free access, they then left their users to sink or swim, and sheltered behind the philosophy that it was wrong to ' spoonfeed '.

The first need in an open access library is to provide directional guides: large, clear, comprehensive signs in all key traffic areas (vestibule, lift lobbies, stairways) stating what each floor houses, and where main subjects are shelved. It is also useful to display a large plan or model of the library's layout. It is equally important to guide the bookstacks effectively and in detail. All these guides should be of a professional standard and appearance; the days of the well-meaning amateur with his stencil-brush or felt-tip pen are surely over—the library's readers are after all accustomed to high standards everywhere else, in shops, supermarkets, airports. Amateurism has no charm in this context, and amounts indeed to very poor public relations.

What is also desirable is to prepare annually a brief printed handbook or guide to the library and its services, a copy of which can be given to every library user. This handbook or guide should be as attractively produced as possible, well written, and should contain the following information:

1 A list of library staff members, stating the areas or services for which they are responsible, and indicating where they are to be found in the library building and what their internal telephone numbers are.

2 A section of general information, including hours of opening and details of enrolment and membership.

3 A diagram and/or description of the general layout of the library, mentioning any branches which exist.

4 A more detailed account of the arrangement of the collections, intemizing and describing special types and categories.

5 A note on the public catalogues available; their arrangement; and how to use them.

6 A full account of the various services the library offers: reference services; loan facilities; book reservation; photocopying and photographic services; and so on.

7 The official text of the library's rules and regulations.

Apart from this general guide, there is scope also for various subject guides: perhaps, as at Reading University, by faculty—arts, science, agriculture. In these much more detailed information can be given about materials and bibliographical tools available. Most libraries, in addition, try to produce book-lists and catalogues of various kinds: the commonest being a list of current periodicals available in the library, and a regular list of accessions.

A library will also display a number of general notices. Inevitably, some of these will have to be prohibitive—'Do not smoke', for example—but the aim should be to keep these to the absolute minimum. More important are the notices offering help: 'Please ask for the books you need' belongs to this category, and crystallizes what should be the library's whole philosophy.

It is essential in an academic library that readers be offered instruction in its use. The *Report of the Committee on Libraries* refers to the ' widespread ignorance ' among students with regard to the tools and services a library provides. The report also notes that the amount and nature of instruction given to remedy this situation varies greatly between institutions. In the collection *University and research library studies*, edited by W L Saunders, Mavis N Tidmarsh gives a thorough survey of the provision of such instruction in academic libraries.

Reader instruction, to be effective, must be offered at a number of different levels. The first involves introducing new students to the library, and this can be done in quite a variety of ways. A standard element is an introductory and welcoming talk to new students in one or more large groups by the university librarian himself—usually in the students' first week. This should be supplemented subsequently by the distribution of the printed guide or handbook to the library, and by arranging a series of conducted tours of the library. These tours should be short, in groups not exceeding a dozen or so students, and most members of the library staff will be needed to act as guides. Various visual devices have been used as substitutes for or additions to the introductory talk and the conducted tour: a film of the library and its services (as at Southampton), or a video-tape (as at Sussex).

The next stage of reader instruction is, in the words of the Parry Report, ' guidance on the literature in the student's subject, with specific instruction in the use of bibliographical tools '. The Parry Report notes that the form of such instruction should include seminars and lectures, and stresses that the timing of it should be given very careful consideration, avoiding the beginning of the academic year (which would be too early in the student's career). The seminar method, for example, has been used at Southampton and Reading; the system at the latter was described by Dr Hazel Mews in her article *Library instruction to students at the University of Reading* as follows: ' Two seminars were arranged for all first-year students . . .; the pairs of seminars followed a general pattern with individual variations. The first seminar was concerned primarily with imparting general information about the organization of a library, with explaining the classification scheme (Dewey), with demonstrating the use of the catalogues, the handling of bibliographies, reference books etc, and with a visit to relevant shelves in the library. At the end of this seminar each student was given a set of search problems or exercises and assigned one of these to undertake before the next seminar. The second seminar consisted of a discussion of the methods by which the students had found, or sought to find, the answers to the questions posed, and of any incidental problems they had encountered. As each student had been assigned a different problem this discussion was designed to give all the students in the group the opportunity of sharing the experiences of those who had worked on the other problems. These exercises have remained an integral part of the Reading University Library instruction programme since 1965, although they have been considerably revised and expanded. Their object is to induce the student to use the library catalogues, to confront a few of the unfamiliar problems connected with the shelving of folio books, pamphlets etc, to use books as tools for finding information, to make acquaintance with some standard bibliographies and to acquire care and precision in giving bibliographical references. They are drawn up by subject specialists on the library staff or those with long experience of information work and they are in some cases the result of consultation with lecturers in the relevant departments.' This stage of instruction can be given in a student's first or second year.

The final stage of reader instruction is that geared to the needs of postgraduate students. Again this can be in the form of seminars, arranged preferably in co-operation with the teaching staff; and of course, it can also be on an individual basis between the postgraduate himself and a suitably qualified member of the library staff. There will also be instructional courses outside the postgraduate's own university which he can be encouraged to attend: those run by the National Lending Library for Science and Technology, for example.

The foregoing records the essential pattern of reader instruction, but it would be wrong to give the impression that there is anything cut-and-dried about the topic. This area of library endeavour is littered with false starts and total failures. The root reason is that librarians are as yet unaccustomed to teaching, and too often forget that what they are trying to do is to produce, not librarians like themselves, but library-orientated students. The human, psychological, aspects of reader instruction merit a great deal of further study and consideration. Too vigorous and insensitive an approach creates an amount of antagonism out of all proportion to whatever gains might come from the instruction itself. Reading's mistake, for example, was to have the seminars made compulsory; quite apart from the resentment this caused among students, it proved too ambitious a project in terms of library staff time. Other errors were that the timing was wrong (being early in a student's first year); that the teaching staff and the academic departments were not fully consulted and involved; and that insufficient attention was paid to the latter stages of a student's career. Similar mistakes have been made, and are being made, elsewhere, not all of them, unfortunately, recognized as such. Reader instruction is something which must be evolved carefully; it cannot spring forth fully-formed. This is no excuse for not providing it; it is absolutely essential. But done badly, it can seriously harm the library's reputation within its academic community.

In her book *Reader instruction in colleges and universities*, Dr Mews sets out the questions a librarian must ask himself before planning reader instruction courses. The most important of these are:

1) Are the teaching staff interested in such instruction, and do they believe it to have value?

2) Do the teaching staff wish to give the instruction themselves, or to co-operate with the library staff in giving it, or leave it entirely to the library staff?

3) How should the library make its first approaches: to faculty boards, or to departments, or to individuals, and how formally?

4) At what levels do students need instruction?

5) Will students be reluctant to receive instruction, and if so, how can their reluctance be overcome?

6) Will the library staff welcome the idea?

7) Are there enough competent assistants to tackle the work?

8) Can it be done by library staff in addition to their other duties, and/or must provision for new staff be made?

9) What would be the content of the courses?

10) What methods of teaching should be used: lectures, tutorials, seminars, audio-visual equipment?

11) Where should the instruction take place: in the library, or in departments, or in some central room or lecture-hall?

12) When should the instruction take place: in which student year, and at what times in the timetable?

PHOTOCOPYING AND PHOTOGRAPHIC SERVICES

Every university library now has available one or more photocopying machines, and the facility of such machines to reproduce quickly and conveniently well-nigh perfect copies of parts of books, periodical articles, and documents and records, has caused a minor revolution. It has revolutionized library loans, especially inter-library loans: to have a photocopy made of an article from a journal is often very much less trouble than borrowing it. As far as scholars and researchers are concerned, it has removed the chore of manual transcription. It has increased the availability of texts for teaching purposes. It has had its effect, too, on library routines: all sorts of records (lists of overdues, lists of desiderata, catalogue records) can be manufactured easily in any number of copies.

The very large range of possibilities offered by photocopying machines has, on the other hand, brought problems also. The greatest of these is the problem of copyright. A library just cannot go ahead and reproduce copyright material just as it likes. It has to operate within the law. Consequently, it is a standard and obligatory procedure for every photocopying transaction which involves copyright text that the person who is to be the recipient of the copy made by the library must sign a copyright declaration form which states that the copy is strictly for the purposes of research or private study; also, only a single copy can be made, and the amount of text copied must not exceed a reasonable proportion of the book or journal. The other major problem is to do with the financial control of a photocopying service. Some libraries still try within their own academic community (at least as far as academic staff are concerned) to operate a ' free ' service from library funds; but this eventually creates something of a runaway budget. Other libraries make a standard charge per sheet to every user, or provide coin-operated machines. The aim should never be to make a profit—since it is such a key service—but either to break even, or to keep within a modest (that is, in relation to the library's overall budget) financial allocation.

Despite the problems mentioned, it is an essential reader service to provide adequate and efficient photocopying arrangements. There should be sufficient machines, and machines of sufficient capacity, to obviate photocopying delays. The choice of machines, and their location, deserve particular consideration.

Some university libraries (Senate House, London, for example; Southampton and Reading) also provide a general photographic service. Often this is the university's photographic service, but housed under the library's roof. Such a service makes slides and prints from books and manuscripts; it also photographs paintings and museum objects; and it does 'location work'—that is, the photographers go out and photograph buildings, for example. In general, it provides the visual aids required by the university for teaching and research. There is no essential reason why such a service should be part of the library. There are indeed certain advantages: the library is itself a central service, usually in a central location, and this makes for convenience; and it is a safer situation where library materials do not have to leave the library premises to be photographed. But if, for example, a university sets up a central printing service, it would make much more sense if the university's photographic service was integrated with it, rather than left under the library's care.

NEW MEDIA

It must always be remembered that the book is not the only means of storing and disseminating information. As Richard Fothergill points out in his report *A challenge for librarians?* the new situation which is evolving in education is that ' the book is being supplemented but not superseded by other formats of material ' (for example, films, film-strips, language tapes, gramophone records, video tapes, slides; and under this heading, too, comes the installation in libraries of closed circuit television systems).

The reason for the development, in Fothergill's view, is plain enough: ' In primary schools and increasingly in secondary schools, the tendency towards supplying individual students with materials with which to work independently or in small groups is growing, and the result is that future students at our universities and other forms of higher education are going to expect the same methods of teaching and learning when they arrive there '. And what the development means in library terms has been expressed in the 1970-71 report of the University of Surrey's Institute for Educational Technology, *Self-teaching systems in university science courses*, as follows: ' It is obvious that the library of the future will not be just a book collection, but will handle many other audio-visual materials designed for use in self-teaching situations '. As Ellsworth also says (in Brown: *Planning the academic library*): 'Audio-visual developments . . . are going to play a role that will make the library very different '.

Already the increasing use of audio-visual materials has presented new problems of organization and exploitation. Janet Andrew, in her foreword to Fothergill's report, notes that: 'A few collections have been fully integrated into the library and catalogued and classified along with the printed materials, whilst the others have been developed separately in resource centres '.

In a paper given to a conference on new media at the University of Surrey at the end of 1971, and subsequently and in more detail in his book *New media and the library in education*, Dr B J Enright has noted the choices open to a librarian in relation to new media and the attendant difficulties.

The choices are three:

1) To decide to exclude the new materials, making them the responsibility of another section of the university and not of the library.

2) To acquire and store media materials, but to keep them in a separate part of the library.

3) To co-ordinate books and non-book materials fully, even inter-mingling them.

Enright himself prefers the last, but concedes that the second is an easier solution.

The difficulties connected with introducing non-book materials into libraries, in Enright's view, arise because (i) by virtue of their training the thinking of all librarians is dominated by the book; (ii) conventional library problems are difficult enough without adding this further type of material; (iii) librarians tend to be suspicious of

5

media and media specialists; (iv) there is a lack of multi-media library procedures; (v) materials and equipment are costly; (vi) the physical form of the material causes problems from the storage and arrangement point of view; (vii) non-books become obsolescent at a more rapid rate than books; (viii) the availability and content of non-book materials is poorly documented; and (ix) copyright problems relating to non-book materials are more complex and intractable.

Many librarians feel that the actual production of audio-visual materials should be quite separate from library operations. Some doubt that books and non-books will mix, but in a limited way this is already happening quite successfully: at Surrey University for example, where tape-slide productions are available to students for use in the library (see plate 8). However, the librarian must remember that books will remain his main concern for many years; he must not spreadeagle his energies and his resources just because, being already a central service in his university, he feels he must therefore attract to himself every other central service.

A prudent summing-up of the whole matter is provided in the Library Association's policy statement on university libraries and learning resources: ' The degree of involvement of libraries in non-book materials will vary from university to university according to local circumstances; at one extreme, the librarian may be represented on appropriate committees, at the other, all audio visual operations may be placed under the librarian. What is essential is that the library should be involved, both at a policy-making and an operational level '.

HOURS OF OPENING

As a conclusion to this account of the reader services offered by a university library, some comment is required on the number of hours such services should be available. A university does not maintain a nine-to-five five-day week, and neither should its library. Students and academic staff are just as likely to want to use its facilities in the evenings and at weekends as they are to use them during the day. It is therefore imperative that a library maintain generous hours of opening during term time: the minimum should be from about nine in the morning until ten at night on week-days, and on Saturday and

Sunday afternoons. This is not merely because the library must now be recognized as an active and vital university service rather than as a museum or storehouse, but also because, as will have become evident from most of this book so far, it represents a massive university investment, and it would be inappropriate to reduce the potential of such an investment by limiting its hours of availability.

Long hours, of course, do not mean that a complete library service must be offered during every one of those hours. No more is required in the evenings and at weekends than access to books and reading places and minimum staffing.

VII

UNIVERSITY LIBRARY BUILDINGS

FLEXIBILITY

The great expansion of university education in the past decade has naturally resulted in a vast amount of university building. New campuses have sprung up in many places; older universities, without exception, have increased in size: many have doubled in size. A by-product of such universal expansion has been the appearance of a host of new university library buildings. These newcomers are radically different from any that preceded them, because the basic aim of their design has been to achieve flexibility.

Previously, university libraries were monumental, characterized (as Henry Faulkner Brown notes in his article *University library buildings* and Keyes Metcalf in his book *Planning academic and research library buildings*) by lofty reading-rooms, massive interior walls, and multi-tier bookstacks of low ceiling height. Their external appearance, and their entrance halls and stairways, were meant to impress: a good example here is the neo-Gothic building designed by Sir Gilbert Scott (as a dummy run for St Pancras Railway Station, according to wry local legend) which formerly housed the library at Glasgow University (see plate 4: the Gilbert Scott building is on the left of the picture, contrasting with the new library building on the right). The major defect of such buildings was that they were fixed function: that is, each area was designed to meet one specific functional or operational need and there was no possibility of interchange. A reading-room could only be a reading-room, and a bookstack only a bookstack.

This kind of inflexibility might have been defensible in less expansionist times, but the situation today demands that any new library building must, above all else, be flexible. E R S Fifoot in his article *University library buildings* defines flexibility as follows: ' In library terms it means the interchangeability—not overnight, but over the

128

summer vacation—of all major stack areas, reading areas, and staff areas. This implies a building which can bear stack loads throughout, which will light and ventilate a large number of readers anywhere, a building with no interior loadbearing walls, and a building whose services and other fixed elements are grouped so as to free the largest area on each floor for changing library use. I would go further and require the building and all its individual areas to be rectangular.' Such functional considerations are, of course, the main reason for the rather ordinary external appearance of most modern library buildings: we have jumped from neo-Gothic monuments to glorified shoe-boxes. A modern library can readily be mistaken for an office block or a warehouse. Since emphasis on purely functional considerations tends to result in (to quote the expressions of the *Architectural review*'s critic J M R in his article on Glasgow University Library, *The new climax to the Glasgow skyline*) ' a somewhat dumpy building mass ' or ' lumpish cube ', and since governmental tight-fistedness does not leave any money over for expensive finishes or aesthetic additions, architects have been driven to rather desperate attempts to improve the outward appearance of library buildings. Such attempts range from experiments with fenestration (hence the prevalence of arrow-slit windows all over university campuses, as though the university were expecting a siege and had trained its staff in toxophily) to much bolder approaches, such as that at Glasgow University where the architect of the new library, while retaining the lumpish cube for the main library areas, has placed service areas in towers of different heights (see plate 4) to achieve a more distinctive visual effect.

The flexibility described by E R S Fifoot is best obtained by building a library according to the modular system. This system has been pioneered by Angus Snead MacDonald, Ralph Ellsworth, and Keyes Metcalf, and is described by the latter as follows: ' Under the modular system . . . a building is supported by columns placed at regular intervals. Nothing within the building is weight-bearing except the columns, though the outside walls may be. It follows in theory that nothing within the building is fixed and immovable except the columns, though in fact it is generally impracticable if not impossible to shift the location of stairways, elevators, heating facilities, ducts, and plumbing.

'A rectangle—usually, but not always, a square—defined by four adjacent columns, is known as a *bay*. The modular building, then, is made up of identical bays, any one of which may be furnished as part of a reading area, filled with ranges of shelving, or divided by partitions into offices; or combinations of two or even three of these may be used. No difficult structural alterations are required when a bay that has been serving one of these purposes is assigned to another.'

Metcalf sums up the advantages of the modular system by saying that ' a building consisting largely of space that can be used for almost any purpose without extensive or expensive alterations should in the long run save money and prevent complications which so often arise as space requirements change '. He does comment, though, that the modular system is not without its faults. The most fundamental of these, according to Metcalf, is that no one column spacing or bay size is ideal for all purposes: what is an ideal module for bookstack will not be equally ideal for another function. Other faults of the system are obvious to any visitor to a modular library. One is that the columns demanded by the system are rarely unobtrusive; in extreme cases, indeed, they offend both eye and convenience (a column occurring right in the middle of an office is not unheard of, for example). Another is that the rigorous application of a standard module seems often to rob the architect of the chance to achieve handsome proportions in a building: it is a shock to realize on entering an older building with good proportions how infrequently this agreeable quality is to be found in modular structures.

However, none of the faults of the modular system outweigh in importance its essential merit of flexibility, and this is why the application of the system to library buildings in this country has become almost standard. The module used varies, but as K A Lodewycks notes in his book *Essentials of library planning*, 'A column spacing of between $22\frac{1}{2}$ to 23 feet from centre to centre depending on the thickness of the columns, will offer no obstruction to the proper arrangement of bookshelves, tables, card cabinets and other types of equipment used in libraries '. Lodewycks also comments that there is a trend towards uniformity in the remaining dimension: ceiling height. Ceiling height should be low enough to be economically employed for book storage at any point: ' For example, an eight foot ceiling height provides adequate clearance for light fittings above a standard 7 foot 6 inch tier of bookshelving and is regarded as comfortable for a reading or work area provided the area is limited in size or is broken up with shelving or screening here and there '. The proviso in the last few words of this statement is worth noting. In Edinburgh University's new library, built according to the modular system and with a standard ceiling height of eight feet, the major reading areas have had to be divided and humanized by curtains and potted plants.

Complete flexibility in a library building requires more than the application of a uniform module. There should also be uniform standards of lighting, ventilation and flooring if absolute interchangeability is the aim. Anyone who has been involved in adjustments to the older, more inflexible type of library building will be all too familiar with the routine of first, move your bookstack, and secondly, call the university electrician to re-arrange the light-fittings. With lighting, the aim should be to provide a uniform distribution, avoiding sharp contrasts; and most library planners point out that daylight must not be relied upon. Good ventilation is essential. E R S Fifoot in the article mentioned earlier, stresses that: ' To construct a building in which books even thirty years old are to be preserved, without air-conditioning, is to waste public money . . . It is inescapable that it is a national economy fully to air-condition all university libraries.' Finally, it is plainly convenient to have uniform flooring if ready interchangeability is the aim; however, equally plainly, this is not as important as an overall standard of lighting and ventilation, and it must be acknowledged that if bookstack is converted to reading-space it would be a very unusual type of flooring that did not need some amount of repair or renewal.

ENTRANCE AREA

The foregoing section has been concerned with the library building overall: its appearance, functional flexibility, lighting and ventilation. It must next be examined with regard to the basic elements of which it is composed. These fall into three main groups: the entrance area; the processing departments; the space for books and the places for readers.

The entrance area of a library is, in the words of R E Ellsworth (*Planning the college and university library building: a book for campus planners and architects*), 'the introduction to the building', and as such is vital. Its main components are the following:

i) vestibule
ii) cloakrooms and lavatories
iii) issue desk services
iv) reference services
v) catalogues
vi) stairways and lifts to the rest of the library.

All of these are perfectly illustrated in the photograph (plate 5 and dustjacket) of the entrance area at Reading University Library. The upper right of the picture shows the doors of the main entrance, leading into the vestibule. All one side of the vestibule is given over to cloakroom accommodation, with male lavatories on one side (the door to these, which are to the left of the main doors, is just visible in the photograph) and female lavatories on the other (off the picture). It will be seen that part of the cloakroom accommodation is staffed by an attendant: the area of cloakroom on the attendant's far right is unmanned. Cloakroom accommodation is essential not merely from the point of view of the readers' convenience, which is obvious enough, but also from the point of view of library security; in order to avoid book-losses it is necessary to oblige readers to deposit coats and cases outside the main library area. To offer readers maximum security for their possessions, an attendant is provided; he gives a tag for items deposited with him, and stays guard over them. However, for the reader who is in too much of a hurry to hand over belongings to the attendant, receive a tag, and retrieve them from him subsequently, unmanned cloakroom space is provided also. On the whole, readers seem to prefer expediency to security, and the amount of unmanned accommodation provided is now greater than the superintended area.

From the vestibule the user passes through the control wicket to the main hall of the library. This control point also is the one and only exit from the main part of the library: all books must be shown by readers as they leave to the assistant stationed there, and all books which are to be borrowed from the library are stamped and issued by the assistant.

However, to return to the user who is entering the library: once he has passed through the control wicket he is confronted by what Ellsworth calls 'the library keys', explaining these as follows: 'Immediately beyond the lobby one should see the tools and services that serve as keys to the library. People who come into a library consist of two groups: those who know where the books (or place they want to study) are, and those who don't. Those who know should find stairways readily accessible once they have passed the lobby. Those who don't know will want to use an information desk, the card catalog, the circulation desk, and the reference services to help them find their materials. Therefore these services should be visible to the reader as soon as he enters the library.'

Ellsworth's 'keys' are clearly depicted in the photograph. The stairways (one in the middle of the picture, and part of the other visible in the foreground) are boldly placed for those who know what they want and where they want to go; also available (off the left of the picture) are lifts to the upper floors of the library. For the others, there is the circulation and information desk directly in front of them (on the extreme left of the picture), the card catalogues (at the top of the picture) and reference books around the walls. These then, along with the vestibule and cloakroom accommodation, are the essential ingredients of an entrance area.

PROCESSING DEPARTMENTS

The next group of elements are the processing departments. Ellsworth, having dealt with the entrance functions of a library building, continues: 'The layout, design and placing of these functions constitutes a problem that is unique to libraries for the reason that not only must each function have the right space relationship to the other functions, but also to the technical processes. This situation exists because adding publications to the library and cataloguing them involves very frequent use of the card catalog and reference tools. Much valuable time will be lost unless the walking distance is short.'

Thus the processing departments of a library tend to be grouped around the perimeter of the main hall, as are the administrative offices. The cataloguing department at Reading, for example, has a door opening off from the public catalogue area. The acquisitions department should also be on this perimeter, alongside the cataloguing department, and again having convenient access to the public catalogues and the reference works (which of course include the essential tools for acquisitions work: printed catalogues and bibliographies). Also on the perimeter should be the accommodation required for the receipt and despatch of books and other library materials; and the preparations department. Ellsworth also recommends that the periodicals department should be here, but the location of this department depends on how periodicals are displayed. If there is a current periodicals room on another floor (on the first floor, for example at Reading), then that is where the periodicals department should be also. Other sections—the library bindery, for example—need not be here; often the basement of the library is a suitable location.

SPACE FOR BOOKS AND PLACES FOR READERS

In a nutshell, the basic arrangement of a library is to group compactly the entrance and processing areas, to use the basement for storage purposes and non-public services, and to devote the remaining floors of the building to the provision of space for books and places for readers. This is why there is much to support the idea that, if a library building is (as it usually is) a multi-storey structure, the central entrance and processing area should occur not at the base of the structure, on the ground floor, but at a middle level, thereby reducing the distance the user has to travel to the book and reading floors: that is, in a library building with eight storeys of books and reading provision, instead of obliging the user to ascend anything up to eight floors to find what he needs, to place the entrance in the middle would give him a maximum of only four floors to go up or down.

Calculating the amount of space required for books and readers is the essential sum for the library planner. Of course, he does not plan for his present number of books and readers: he needs to plan for what these figures will be several years ahead. It is not usually difficult for him to predict the future size of his stock, which he bases mainly on the trend of his current accessions rate; and he is usually able to establish from the university what the future growth in student numbers is likely to be. He then applies a standard formula to convert these needs into square footage. The usual formula for a rough estimate is to assign 25 square feet for each reader; 60 square feet for each 1,000 volumes; and having added square footage for library staff (100 square feet per person), to allow a further 40 percent for all other purposes (stairways, corridors, and so on). In this way he arrives at the approximate size of the building, and by applying whatever is the current UGC formula as to price per square foot, arrive also at its probable cost.

Considerable variety is possible, and indeed essential, in the matter of providing space for books and places for readers. The traditional pattern was to segregate the two, confining most of the library's stock to high-density bookstack areas, and most of its readers to large reading-rooms. An example of this basic pattern, though not too rigidly applied, may be seen at Reading University Library. Students are expected to use one of the two large reading-rooms (see plate 6), sharing multi-seat tables; the only seating provided in the bookstack areas are the tables on its periphery (see plate 7). This kind of division is becoming less frequent, the aim now being to integrate books and readers to a much greater extent. There are of course exceptions to this: for example, the storage areas for less-used books are not usually provided with reader-places. Such areas, in any case, are usually located in the basement of the library building, and the most effective type of shelving to use for this sort of storage is of the ' compact ' kind: that is, bookstacks in this category (in the words of the *Architects' journal information sheet 1592*, 28th February 1968) ' have complete ranges mounted on rails running transversely to the direction of the range; thus enabling the range to be packed closely together for storage but moved along the rails to open an aisle for access to the books in any desired position '; the movement of such ranges can be either manual or mechanical or both.

Seating provision as such has moved away from the tradition of the large library table. These must still be provided, but many readers prefer individual tables (usually two foot by three foot); and apart from large and small tables grouped in reading areas and ranged around the perimeter of each floor, seating is also provided in carrels (that is, enclosed individual reading-places) in various parts of the building, typing carrels, study rooms, and rooms connected with various special collections such as microforms, maps and manuscripts. In main reading-areas, there are many ways of mixing bookstacks and readers. There is what Ellsworth calls the 'checkerboard' system: that is, alternating blocks of bookstack with groups of tables for readers. There is also the alcove system, whereby the readers' tables are divided into a series of small groups by bookstacks placed at right-angles to the walls of the room; this system, however, has the disadvantage of often making the classification sequence of the books difficult to follow, and does best where such sequence is not vital—for example, in a collection of roughly-grouped reference books. The best arrangement, however, seems to be the absolutely simple one of placing bookstacks in a block or blocks in the middle of a room, and locating places for readers around its perimeter.

PLANNING PROCEDURES

This chapter has so far dealt with the general principles behind the design of a library building and with the main groups of elements which go to make it up. As a conclusion, some comments are merited on the procedures followed by a university librarian when confronted with the task of planning a new building.

Gelfand divides these procedures into three:
  i) the preparation of a programme
  ii) the development and approval of preliminary plans
  iii) the approval of final plans and specifications.

All of the writers on library buildings mentioned so far stress the importance of the first of these, the programme. Lodewycks defines a programme as a 'preliminary and reasonably complete statement . . . of the library's requirements'. Gelfand observes that it should 'state at the outset the objectives of the institution and their implications for the library service' and then 'describe the plan of library service and state in detail the spatial and technical requirements'. Keyes Metcalf summarizes its purpose as follows:

'1 The preparation of a program is the best way that has been found for the librarian, his staff, and the institution's administration to determine the essential needs of the library and to make all concerned face up to them.

'2 It provides the librarian with an opportunity to point out to the institution's administrative officers and the faculty the physical and, to a lesser extent, the other requirements of the library and to

136

obtain formal approval of this estimate of requirements and of methods to be used in dealing with them. This approval is a matter of first importance.

' 3 It forms the basis on which the architect can plan a satisfactory building.'

Any librarian who has planned or who is trying to obtain a new library building or extend his present building would confirm the truth of Metcalf's first point. Not until a librarian and his staff get down to working out in detail their library's needs with regard to book capacity and places for readers is the actual extent of those needs ever realized; and not until its official committees and bodies receive a costed-out version of such needs does a university grasp the full import of them in university terms. Metcalf's second point follows naturally: the next stage is to persuade the university to approve provision for them. His third point represents the culmination of these negotiations: the placing of the programme in the hands of the architect.

The programme is essential to the architect, because before he can draw up any plans, he must know (as the section on *Inception and primary brief* in the *Architects' journal information library* for 21st February 1968 states):

i) the type of library building required (that is, university, as opposed to national or special or whatever);

ii) the types of service to be provided (for example, lending, reference, research);

iii) the types and quantities of material to be stored (books, periodicals, pamphlets, music, maps, and so on);

iv) the anticipated numbers and types of user and the expected pattern of use;

v) the numbers and types of library staff, with their accommodation requirements;

vi) the amount of auxiliary accommodation required (cloakrooms, lavatories, and so on);

vii) the anticipated rate of growth of the collection and of the number of readers;

viii) the probability of future changes within the library.

Next comes the second stage of planning procedure, as indicated by Gelfand. The architect, having studied the programme, prepares his outline plans and proposals. For the librarian, this stage can be very easy, or very difficult. Sometimes the architect grasps and interprets the librarian's needs accurately and intelligently, and then there is no problem; the librarian and the architect can get down to actual detail. On other occasions, however, the architect might have launched out erroneously on his own, ignoring functional considerations held by the librarian to be basic: in which case, the architect has to be persuaded to start again, or the librarian will end up with what will be from his point of view a totally unsatisfactory building.

When the architect's outline proposals have been accepted by the librarian, there will then follow the final stage, that of establishing and approving detailed specifications. If the previous stages can be counted as being difficult, this final stage must be regarded as the most arduous of all. Months and months of work are required both on the part of the architect and on the part of the librarian. The list of topics for detailed consideration at times appears almost endless—the design of special areas; the apportioning of office accommodation; the lay-out of bookstack and reading-areas; the choice and location of furniture and equipment; the placing of telephones—since not only are major aspects involved but also a welter of minutiae. Before all of this has been completed, building will have begun, so that the constant library staff conferences over particular details will be interspersed by at least a few visits (architects and contractors are very chary about allowing such visits, since experience has taught them it is best to debar the client from wandering the site) to the growing shell of the new library: where the librarian is wont to stand cold and uncomfortable among the concrete and cables and wonder if it was all a mistake.

However, when the building is finally completed (usually after the library staff and stock have moved into it), there is every reason to expect—if all the essential principles and procedures outlined in this chapter have been followed—that it will be a success not only on its opening day but also for years to come. Most writers on library buildings feel that an absolute guarantee of this can be obtained only if a university is wise enough to appoint a Library building consultant to assist the university librarian in his planning. Every librarian is willing

138

to expend a vast amount of time, patience and trouble over conceiving and designing a new library; but no matter how much expertise and knowledge he amasses, he would still benefit from the advice of such a consultant.

VIII

CO-OPERATION

TYPES OF CO-OPERATIVE ACTIVITY: Formally-organized co-operation between university libraries in Britain began in 1925, with a Conference on Library Co-operation held under the auspices of the Association of University Teachers, and attended by members of the Library Co-operation Committee of that body and by a number of academic librarians. The conference resolved to regularize the routines of loans between university libraries, to set up an enquiry office, and to elect a joint standing committee with executive powers to carry out its policy.

If the need for co-operation between university libraries was evident then, the intervening years have only served to emphasize the need. In the words of the Parry Report: 'In estimating the efficiency of a university library one can make the broad assertion that it should be able to meet all the needs of undergraduates from its own stock, and as many as possible of the needs of its research workers. Where research is concerned, however, there is a margin of inability which is inevitable. In view of the highly-specialised nature of some of the research work done, the age and scarcity of some of the material required in the humanities, and the ever-increasing amount of information (largely in periodical form and from foreign countries) demanded in the sciences, no university library can contemplate attaining self-sufficiency. This limitation has always been accepted by the libraries, and means have been devised for overcoming it and ensuring that it imposes the minimum disability on the academic researcher. Now more than ever, with the increase in the number of academic people engaged in research and the mounting costs of books and periodicals, it has become necessary to explore all the means whereby a university library can co-operate with other libraries without impairing its own efficiency—indeed with a view to extending and improving its own services.' It should be noted that these remarks apply to every size of library. As

Gelfand notes, ' Even the largest libraries must engage in co-operative activities to augment their resources, for today it is impossible for any library to be absolutely comprehensive in all fields '.

The main types of co-operative activity are the following:

    i) Inter-library lending
    ii) Joint publications
   iii) Inter-library study facilities
   iv) Co-operative acquisitions schemes
    v) Co-operative and centralized cataloguing
   vi) Co-operative storage schemes
  vii) Transfer of materials
 viii) Regional co-operation
   ix) Library research
    x) Professional associations

Co-operative and centralized cataloguing (v) has already been dealt with, in the relevant section of chapter V; as have co-operative storage schemes (vi) in the section of chapter IV on little-used materials.

INTER-LIBRARY LENDING

Of all the types of co-operative activity, inter-library lending is the most important. After the Conference on Library Co-operation mentioned earlier, an Enquiry Office to deal with inter-library loans was accordingly set up, at Birmingham University. This Office commenced work on March 1st 1925, and was eventually transferred to the National Central Library.

The National Central Library began in 1916, as the Central Library for Students. It was supported financially by grants from the Carnegie United Kingdom Trust and its main purpose was to lend books to adult education students. Following the recommendation of the Kenyon Committee on Public Libraries (*Report on public libraries in England and Wales*, 1927) that it should be developed as the central clearing-house of a national inter-lending network, the library was in 1931 incorporated by Royal Charter as the National Central Library. It was governed by a Board of eleven Trustees, two of whom were appointed by the Trustees of the British Museum, one by the Trustees of the British Museum (Natural History), and one by the Library Association; these four Trustees in turn appointed the other seven. An

141

6

Executive Committee of twenty-five members was responsible for the management of the library.

The Parry Report described the National Central Library as 'the pivot of the inter-library lending scheme for England and Wales'. It was also, as Woledge and Page note, 'the intermediary in the important service of loans between British and foreign libraries'. In the year ending 31st March 1968, applications from all types of library to borrow books and periodicals totalled 141,977. The total number of loans made by the National Central Library, or through its agency, to university libraries was 34,676; loans by university libraries at the direct request of the National Central Library totalled 31,791. As noted in the *Report of the National Libraries Committee*, most of the material requested by university libraries from the National Central Library was either foreign material or older British publications in the humanities or social sciences, requests for scientific and technical publications going to the National Lending Library for Science and Technology. The National Central Library maintained union catalogues of the holdings of university libraries, regional library systems and 391 special ('Outlier') libraries which had agreed to lend through its agency; thus a loan request from one library was despatched by the NCL to whichever other library was shown in the union catalogues as possessing that item. The loaning library then sent the item direct to the borrowing library. Though the NCL's union catalogues contained approximately two and a half million entries, they had as locating tools a number of serious limitations, which the Dainton Report summarized as follows:

'(i) The holding library is not shown on entries lodged by regional library systems.

(ii) There are arrears of over one million items for inclusion in the catalogues, due very largely to staff shortages and the labour involved in making out catalogue card entries.

(iii) Many libraries are slow to notify the NCL of additions to, and deletions from, their stocks.

(iv) Some material included in the union catalogues proves not to be available for loan when requested.'

The National Central Library was able to supply some of the items requested from its own stock, but this proportion was very small—

' only about 12 percent of university applications can be satisfied from it ', according to the Parry Report. The overall result of the NCL's difficulties with its union catalogues, and the comparative smallness of its own stock (even though, for example, the NCL has since 1968 begun to obtain for its loan collection nearly all non-scientific books from American university presses on publication), was one of some degree of failure and delay in its meeting loan requests. A six-month survey conducted on behalf of the Parry Committee revealed that of 13,958 loan requests from university libraries, only 10,613, or 76 percent, were satisfied. As for delays, the Parry Committee found as follows: ' Of the items for which supply time was known (which was 83 percent of all requests) 10 percent were supplied by return . . .; 31 percent later, but within one week; 26 percent later, but within two weeks; and 33 percent after two weeks. Cumulatively, 41 percent of requests were met by the end of one week, and 67 percent by the end of two weeks. There were extremely long delays for some of the remaining 33 percent, 8·6 percent of which took over 6 weeks. These figures denote the delay about which complaints have been made to us by users of the service. In addition, considerable irritation is caused when after a long delay, borrowers are eventually told that the book is not available.'

In 1973 the National Central Library, as recommended by the Dainton Report, became part of the lending wing of the British Library, at Boston Spa in Yorkshire, the headquarters of the National Lending Library for Science and Technology.

The background of the National Lending Library for Science and Technology is succinctly described in Chapter V of the Dainton report: ' In 1954, the Advisory Council on Scientific Policy recommended the creation of a national science lending library to take over and develop the postal lending service which the Science Museum Library was operating in South Kensington. The recommendation was influenced partly by the severe limitations of the South Kensington site and partly by the Science Museum Library's difficulty in combining successfully its growing postal lending operations with a public reference service and its lending services to local institutions . . . Planning of the new library commenced in 1956 on the instructions of the Department of Scientific and Industrial Research (DSIR). It was intended that the new library should have adequate coverage of all scientific literature relevant to research and that it should give the quickest possible service, by having an organization designed specifically for a lending function and by eliminating as far as possible waiting lists and delays due to binding. Surveys of the postal services led to the selection of a 60-acre site for the new library at Boston Spa in Yorkshire, from which virtually all parts of the United Kingdom can be reached by post within twenty-four hours. In August 1962 the National Lending Library for Science and Technology (NLLST) became fully operational.'

The Director of the NLLST, Dr D J Urquhart, in his article *The National Lending Library, 1968,* notes that the library's collection of current serials then numbered 31,904 titles; and that the total of loan and photocopy requests dealt with had increased from 404,400 in 1965 to 779,000 in 1968. In addition to scientific and technical periodicals, the NLLST also now stocks social science serials, and by April 1968, was able to supply 80 percent of the items requested. Its overall success in meeting requests for scientific and technical publications is about 90 percent, and all straightforward requests are dealt with on the day they are received. Dr Urquhart considers that the reasons for the success of NLLST's system lie in his abandonment of the concept of a union catalogue, and of the ' deeply ingrained tradition ' of the author record: the NLLST files everything by title. The NLLST, in fact, operates with the approach and efficiency of a mail-order firm.

Apart from borrowing through the National Central Library and the NLLST, university libraries also borrow from each other direct. Such direct borrowing is largely on the basis of the *British union-catalogue of periodicals* (BUCOP). The Parry Report states that direct borrowing (under which heading it includes borrowing from the NLLST) amounts to 62 percent of loan applications.

Since inter-library lending is so vital to the success of all types of library, it figured very large in both the Parry and the Dainton reports; and since the greater element of failure lies in dealing with requests for material in the humanities and for foreign materials, it was in these areas that Parry and Dainton were obliged to make their more radical recommendations. The Parry Report recommended that the library departments of the British Museum should become the British

National Library, which should undertake, among other functions, the organization of loans and the maintenance of all types of union catalogues, and the ' responsibility for full coverage of foreign material, either alone or in combination with specialist and university libraries'. The Dainton Report recommended that a new statutory and independent public body, to be known as the National Libraries Authority, should have responsibility for the administration and co-ordination of the work of the British Museum Library, the National Central Library, the National Lending Library for Science and Technology and the British National Bibliography. With particular reference to the National Central Library, it recommended that its loan stocks should be transferred to Boston Spa; and that the highest priority be given to bringing up to date its union catalogues, which should then also be transferred to Boston Spa. Dainton also recommended that the British Museum Library's stock (with the exception of legally-deposited publications) should be available for inter-library lending ' under carefully controlled conditions when photocopying cannot provide a satisfactory solution and when material is not easily available from another library '; and that financial assistance should be available to enable a few larger libraries, such as the university libraries of Oxford and Cambridge, ' to work in particularly close association with the national inter-library lending service '. A minor point, but an important one, is that both Parry and Dainton would like to see telex installed in every university library to help expedite inter-library loan requests.

It will be obvious from the foregoing that inter-library lending is not a cheap service: the Parry committee estimated that each inter-loan costs about £1. It will also be obvious that the larger and richer a particular university library collection is, the greater burden of inter-lending it will bear. And what is equally obvious, but which must not be overlooked by any university librarian, is that inter-library lending should not be allowed to disguise stock deficiencies.

A final point about both the Parry and Dainton reports, but especially the latter, was that their basic theme was the need for co-operation, the need to improve the national network of library resources and services. This was why so much emphasis was laid on the importance of a national library (as in Parry) or a National Libraries Authority (as in Dainton), because in order to achieve an effective national co-operative and inter-lending network it is necessary to have a true national apex to the library system of the country.

Consequently, the recent realization of their proposal for a British Library has been welcomed. Since October 1971, the British Library Organizing Committee and its planning secretariat have been drawing up detailed plans for a national library. A White Paper endorsing the amalgamation of the British Museum Library, the National Reference Library of Science and Invention, the National Central Library, the National Lending Library for Science and Technology and the British National Bibliography was well received by Parliament; and the British Library Act was given formal assent in July 1972. Though reference and bibliographical processing services will be centred in London, the lending wing, as noted earlier, is now located at Boston Spa.

JOINT PUBLICATIONS

The most outstanding example in Britain of joint publication is the *British union-catalogue of periodicals: a record of the periodicals of the world, from the seventeenth century to the present day, in British libraries* (4 vols., 1955-58), with two supplements to 1968, and continued by quarterly and annual cumulations. BUCOP lists over 140,000 titles and indicates where holdings of them exist in approximately 450 libraries. The management of BUCOP is in the hands of a Council, on which university libraries are represented by the Joint Standing Committee on Library Co-operation (mentioned earlier). Since 1962, the National Central Library has been responsible for its publication.

A lesser, but still valuable, example of joint publication is David Ramage's *A finding-list of English books to 1640 in libraries in the British Isles* (1958), which gives locations for some 14,000 *Short-title catalogue* (Pollard and Redgrave) items. This publication was a project of the Standing Conference of National and University Libraries.

INTER-LIBRARY STUDY FACILITIES

This aspect of co-operation, the use by members of one library of the resources of other libraries also, is a logical extension of the idea of all libraries in the country being regarded only as components of what is

146

really a national system. If a student at Sheffield University returns for the summer vacation to his home in Reading, for example, it ought to be (and has been) made possible for him to continue his studies by allowing him to use the library facilities of Reading University. Similarly (and this is a very long tradition) any visiting scholar or researcher must be extended the courtesy of being allowed to use the specialist resources in his field in any university library in the country.

This kind of co-operation also exists between different types of library. In any large city, for example, a high percentage of the seats available in its Reference Library are invariably occupied by university students. Another example, in Edinburgh, is that the National Library is available to students after their second year for material they cannot obtain elsewhere. And the Dainton Report notes that university staff and research students outnumbered all other users of the British Museum Library, forming over two thirds of the total readership in April 1968.

CO-OPERATIVE ACQUISITIONS SCHEMES

No co-operative acquisitions scheme exists among British university libraries as ambitious as America's Farmington Plan, whereby seventy or so libraries, under the sponsorship of the Association of Research Libraries, allied themselves in a project to acquire foreign literature on a national basis, their aim being to ensure that at least one copy of every new publication of interest to research workers in the United States would be obtained by one or other of the libraries taking part in the plan.

The only national acquisitions scheme among British university libraries is the inexpensive and rather half-hearted 'background materials' scheme. In 1952 a sub-committee of the Conference on Library Co-operation investigated the acquisition of pre-1800 books and found that a number of libraries were willing to take part in a co-operative purchase scheme to acquire, by allocating among themselves groups of years between 1600 and 1800, 'background material' (that is, books of secondary interest) of the period. In 1955 the scheme was extended to cover 1550-1599; and it has now been agreed in principle to extend also into the nineteenth century. A catalogue of the books acquired under the scheme is maintained by the National Central Library.

Some progress is also being made by interested libraries in the co-operative acquisition of foreign materials from particular geographical areas. The Standing Conference on Library Materials on Africa (SCOLMA) was set up in 1962 to facilitate the acquisition of library materials needed for African studies. Similar schemes exist or are planned for Asian materials, Slavonic and East European materials, Latin American materials, and materials for American studies; and in all of these cases the Standing Conference of National and University Libraries is actively involved.

TRANSFER OF MATERIALS

Another facet of co-operative attempts to improve library collections is the transfer or redistribution of materials. The prime agent for this in Britain is the British National Book Centre, conducted by the National Central Library. Libraries wishing to dispose of material which though of no use to them might be of use to other libraries inform the BNBC of its availability. The BNBC then circulates lists of items for disposal; interested libraries indicate to the BNBC which items they would like; and the material is sent direct from the donor library to the recipient library. The BNBC also circulates ' wants ' lists.

Since 1948, the BNBC has redistributed about two million items; and since 1960, has sent some 250,000 items to foreign libraries. With regard to the latter, the other side of the coin has been that foreign libraries have sent to the BNBC in their turn more than 50,000 items for distribution among British libraries.

Most university libraries, especially those which have been established only recently, are very appreciative of the BNBC's service in putting their way a further opportunity to augment and improve their stocks. New and impoverished libraries benefit from the surplus largesse of better-endowed institutions; and all libraries with particular specialities and fields of interest are able to rescue items which though insignificant in a general context are valuable in a relevant one.

REGIONAL CO-OPERATION

Regional co-operation is of two kinds. The first is where all, or many types of library in a given region—county, municipal, special, university—co-operate. The second is where a number of libraries of the same type in a particular geographical area co-operate. Both these kinds of co-operation are now common, and both are very much to be encouraged. The Parry Report was quite explicit on this point: ' We recommend that the entire resources of a geographical area should be regarded as a pool from which each individual library could draw. Co-ordination of the resources of libraries would facilitate the extension of coverage and the reduction of expenditure. University libraries within an area should avoid unnecessary and uneconomical duplication of effort and should investigate the advantages of and . . . forms of co-operation.' And the Standing Committee on Libraries of the Committee of Vice-Chancellors and Principals, set up in 1968, has as one of its terms of reference ' the encouragement of inter-library co-operation both between university libraries themselves and between university and public libraries '.

The Parry committee itself investigated four areas—in this case, cities—in respect of co-operation between libraries of different types, and analysed its findings under six headings:

a) *Study facilities*. There was generous co-operation here, as described in an earlier section of this chapter.

b) *Co-operation in acquisitions*. The only ' common feature ' which the committee could establish was the fact that an attempt was made to obviate competition between libraries in a given city with regard to the purchase of certain materials, particularly those of local interest.

c) *Co-operative storage*. There were as yet no examples of this.

d) *Communication*. In only one of the cities (Birmingham) were the university and public libraries linked by telex.

e) *Regular consultation*. Here the committee found that though opportunities for informal contact were plentiful, there was little in the way of established formal relationships.

f) *Staff training*. There was very little inter-change of staffs, and only one example of the provision of classes in librarianship which were attended by junior staff from more than one type of library.

In addition to these six main categories of co-operation, the Parry committee noted co-operation in the creation of union lists of periodicals, the sharing of various technical facilities such as binderies, and the setting up of an information service for the assistance of industry and commerce in the area. The major form of co-operation, as everywhere, was in the inter-loan of library materials. One type of co-operation which the Parry Report does not refer to specifically, but which is becoming quite common, is the setting up of joint computerization projects; an example here is the Birmingham Libraries Co-operative Mechanization Project, in which the librarians of the University of Birmingham, the University of Aston and Birmingham City Libraries have come together to investigate the ways in which their three libraries can jointly use the BNB MARC service, and in particular establish a common machine readable data bank of bibliographic records (see C F Cayless and R T Kimber's article on the project).

It would be wrong to form too poor a picture of the state of regional co-operation between different types of library just because the findings under Parry's six major headings are unimpressive. There is a lot to be said in favour of the much more informal types of co-operation in regions. An example here is the Berkshire Libraries Group, which embraces so many types and sizes of library that large and radical projects—such as co-operative storage and acquisition—would be impossible. However, what is possible is an annual meeting of all concerned, frequent personal contacts between librarians, ready and generous inter-loan arrangements, and the exchange of information about special materials and collections held in each library. This is sufficient to achieve a quite genuine inter-availability of the region's total library resources.

To turn now to the second kind of regional co-operation, that between libraries of the same type. As noted earlier, a particular impetus to co-operation between university libraries themselves has been given by the declared interest in this of the Standing Committee on Libraries of the Committee of Vice-Chancellors and Principals. One of the first examples of regional co-operation between university libraries has been S₃RB, the shorthand name for the co-operative alliance of the university libraries of Southampton, Surrey, Sussex, Reading and Brunel. An examination of the activities of this group will serve to illustrate the possibilities and prospects for such co-operation.

In 1968 the librarians of these universities, which are so geographically placed that all are within an easy drive of each other, agreed to meet to discuss a number of areas of library activity in which co-operation might be possible. The initial meeting was held at Reading University. Subsequent meetings, held at each university library in rotation, the host library acting as convener and secretary, have been of two types: the first, meetings of the chief librarians only, to review progress and suggest future ventures; the second, meetings of working parties of representatives from each library concerned with a specific area of activity. The outcome of these investigations has been extremely gratifying, and the validity of the overall project has now been proved beyond question. In May 1969, the group submitted to the Secretary of the Standing Conference of National and University Libraries, for transmission to the Standing Committee on Libraries of the Committee of Vice-Chancellors and Principals, the following summary of matters being actively pursued:

i) *A directory of resources* to include names of staff concerned with special aspects of the work of the library and to list areas of special strength as well as any special collections.

ii) *Co-operative acquisitions.* At present no more than agreement on a standard form for the interchange of information about expensive works, either announcing intention to purchase or asking if others are intending to purchase. Each library will develop an ' extra-mural' catalogue of specialized and expensive works.

All members stressed the difficulty of co-operation in this area, without similar co-operation in academic planning of courses and new developments.

iii) *Periodical subscriptions.* Agreement to exchange photocopies of contents pages of periodicals, but co-ordination of subscriptions again found to be difficult for reasons as under ii).

iv) *Union list of periodicals.* Agreement to adopt standard format to facilitate production of machine readable entries as the basis for a union catalogue.

v) *Newspapers.* It is hoped to effect considerable economies in storage of newspapers by co-operative microfilming or purchase of microfilms, but finance for necessary labour may prove to be a major difficulty.

vi) *Co-operative purchase of technical processing materials.* Arrangements already concluded for special discounts on large quantity ordering of such items as pamphlet boxes, microfilm boxes, and other special library items.

vii) *Working parties*. Working parties have been set up to deal with the following special areas:

Library instruction and information
Acquisition information
Automation
Periodicals.

LIBRARY RESEARCH

The prime mover in library research in this country has been the Office for Scientific and Technical Information (OSTI). Set up within the Department of Education and Science in 1965, it has awarded over two and a half million pounds in grants and contracts, to promote research into information problems, to develop new techniques and systems, and to improve existing information services and experiment with new ones. Without its assistance, information and library services in the United Kingdom would be far less advanced than they are. Though meant primarily to concern itself only with the scientific and technical field, OSTI has given generous financial assistance to many projects with more general applications: for example, in the field of computerization. Some of the projects have been on the level of extracting sunbeams from cucumbers, but on balance, the overall stimulation of new ideas and approaches brought about by OSTI has more than justified its establishment.

An OSTI-financed project of specific interest to university libraries is the Cambridge University Library Management Research Unit. The Unit was set up in 1968 to study methods leading to increased effectiveness and efficiency in academic libraries, attention being focused on practical investigations making use of O & M techniques rather than on theoretical or abstract approaches. The Director of Research is the Librarian of Cambridge University; there is a team of five in the Unit; and there is a Steering Committee with a representative membership (university libraries, national libraries, OSTI, the Library Association, the Department of Education and Science, and Aslib). The first work undertaken was a survey of university library use by undergraduates; the next major project was concerned with the assessment of administrative effectiveness in academic libraries; and another was a 'failure' survey, to provide librarians with information about the incidence of failure by readers to find wanted books on the shelves. The original grant from OSTI for the Unit terminated in 1972, but the unquestioned success of the work done has led to its renewal.

PROFESSIONAL ASSOCIATIONS

It would be difficult to overestimate the value of the formal and informal meetings of librarians which are brought about automatically by membership of professional associations. Constant and frequent opportunities to exchange information and experience are essential. The inbred library and the inbred librarian belong decidedly to the unlamented past.

The two associations of particular relevance to academic librarianship are first, the University, College and Research Section of the Library Association, and secondly, the Standing Conference of National and University Libraries. The first is open to all members of the Library Association who have an interest in academic librarianship; it has a committee and honorary officers, and holds an annual week-end conference which is always well-attended. The University, College and Research Section provides an excellent chance for the main body of those employed in university libraries to debate their common problems and preoccupations formally and informally.

Membership of the Standing Conference of National and University Libraries is exclusive to chief librarians, though these may send their deputies to its meetings as delegates. SCONUL (as Dr K W Humphreys recounts in his article in *Libri* on its activities) was founded in September 1950, its aim being to provide opportunities for the librarians of 'large learned libraries' to discuss matters of mutual concern, and to represent their views to outside bodies. It is a working conference, meeting twice a year at different universities for just under a week on each occasion. It has a committee consisting of six elected members, the chairman, the vice-chairman, the immediate past-chairman, the honorary treasurer and the executive secretary; and a considerable number of hard-working specialist sub-committees—for example, on buildings, inter-library loans, manuscripts, and shared cataloguing and automation. In addition, it organizes courses and seminars for national and university library staffs, operates a trainee scheme, and arranges exhibitions of foreign books. It now has a membership of fifty-nine university and university college libraries, and ten national libraries.

LIST OF REFERENCES

BOOKS AND PAMPHLETS

ASSOCIATION of Assistant Librarians. South East Division: *Management for librarians*. 1968.

ASSOCIATION of University Teachers: *The university library*. September 1964.

BALMFORTH, C K and COX, N S M: *Interface: library automation with special reference to computing activity*. Newcastle upon Tyne, Oriel Press, 1971.

BOOZ, ALLEN and HAMILTON, *Inc.*: *Problems in university library management*. Washington, DC, Association of Research Libraries, 1970.

BROWN, H F, ed: *Planning the academic library: Metcalf and Ellsworth at York*. Newcastle upon Tyne, Oriel Press, 1971.

BUCK, P: *Libraries and universities: addresses and reports*. Ed by E E Williams. Cambridge, Mass, Belknap Press, Harvard UP, 1964.

The CORNELL *Library Conference papers read at the Dedication of the Central Libraries*, October 1962. Ithaca, New York, Cornell University Library, 1964.

DAVINSON, D: *Academic and legal deposit libraries: an examination guidebook*. London, Bingley, 1965. Second edition 1969.

DOUGHERTY, R M and HEINRITZ, F J: *Scientific management of library operations*. New York, Scarecrow Press, 1966.

ELLSWORTH, R E: *The economics of book storage in college and university libraries*. Metuchen, NJ, Association of Research Libraries and Scarecrow Press, 1969.

ELLSWORTH, R E: *Planning the college and university library building: a book for campus planners and architects*. Boulder, Colorado, Pruett Press, second edition 1968.

ENRIGHT, B J: *New media and the library in education*. London, Bingley, 1972.

FOTHERGILL, R: *A challenge for librarians? A report on the joint* NCET/ASLIB *Audio Visual Group Conference on Multi-Media Resource Organization in Higher Education, held in Hull in December 1970. (Working Paper No. 4).* [*London*], National Council for Educational Technology in association with Aslib Audio Visual Group, 1971.

FRIEDMAN, J and JEFFREYS, A E: *Cataloguing and classification in British university libraries.* University of Sheffield, Postgraduate School of Librarianship, 1967.

FUSSLER, H J and SIMON, J L: *Patterns of use of books in large research libraries.* Chicago, University of Chicago Library, 1961.

GELFAND, M A: *University libraries for developing countries.* Paris, UNESCO, 1968.

The library in the university: the University of Tennessee Library Lectures 1949-1966. Hamden, Conn, Shoe String Press, 1967.

LODEWYCKS, K A: *Essentials of library planning.* Melbourne, University of Melbourne, 1961.

MACLEISH, A: *A time to speak.* Boston, Houghton Mifflin, 1941.

METCALF, K D: *Planning academic and research library buildings.* New York, McGraw-Hill, 1965.

MEWS, H: *Reader instruction in colleges and universities: an introductory handbook.* London, Bingley, 1972.

RAFFEL, J A and SHISHKO, R: *Systematic analysis of university libraries: an application of cost-benefit analysis to the MIT libraries.* Cambridge, Mass, MIT Press, 1969.

RANDALL, W M and GOODRICH, F L D: *Principles of college library administration.* Chicago, American Library Association, second edition 1941.

REPORT *of the National Libraries Committee* (Dainton Report). London, HMSO, 1969.

ROGERS, R D and WEBER, D C: *University library administration.* New York, H W Wilson, 1971.

SAUNDERS, W L ed: *University and research library studies.* Oxford, Pergamon Press, 1968.

SIDNEY, E and BROWN, M: *The skills of interviewing.* London, Tavistock Publications, 1961.

TAYLOR, R S: *The making of a library: the academic library in transition.* New York, Becker & Hayes, 1972.

UNIVERSITY Grants Committee: *Report of the Committee on Libraries* (Parry Report). London, HMSO, 1967.

UNIVERSITY Grants Committee: *Statistics of education, 1969. Volume 6, Universities.* London, HMSO, 1971.

UNIVERSITY Grants Committee: *The University Grants Committee.* London, HMSO, 1970.

WILSON, L R *and* TAUBER, M F: *The university library.* New York, Columbia UP, second edition 1956.

WOLEDGE, G *and* PAGE, B S: *A manual of university and college library practice.* London, Library Association, 1940.

ARTICLES AND PAPERS

BROWN, H F: *University library buildings: library planning (Architects' journal information library,* February 1968).

BROWN, P: *The Bodleian catalogue as machine readable records (Program,* July 1969).

BRUNO, J M: *Decentralization in academic libraries (Library trends,* January 1971).

BURNETT, D: *Economics and the university library (Universities quarterly,* Autumn 1970).

CARMACK, B *and* LOEBER, T: *The library reserve system—another look (College and research libraries,* March 1971).

CAYLESS, C F *and* KIMBER, R T: *The Birmingham libraries cooperative mechanisation project (Program,* July 1969).

DANTON, J P: *The subject specialist in national and university libraries, with special reference to book selection (Libri,* 1967).

DUCHESNE, R M *and* PHILLIPS, A B: *Automation activities in British university libraries: a survey (Program,* July 1971).

ENRIGHT, B J *and* COOPER, J A: *The housekeeping of housekeeping: a library furniture and equipment inventory programme (Program,* January 1969).

FIFOOT, E R S: *University library buildings: a librarian's comments (Architects' journal information library,* March 1968).

FIRST *report of the General Board's Committee on Libraries (Cambridge University reporter,* 28th March 1969).

FOSKETT, D J: *The intellectual and social challenge of the library service (Library Association record,* December 1968).

GOLDHOR, H: *Some thoughts on the curriculum of library schools* (*School and society*, June 1948).

GUTTSMAN, W L: *Subject specialization in academic libraries: some preliminary observations on role conflict and organizational stress* (*Journal of librarianship*, January 1973).

HARO, Robert P: *Change in academic libraries* (*College and research libraries*, March 1972).

HARRAR, H J: *Co-operative storage* (*Library trends*, January 1971).

HAVARD-WILLIAMS, P: *The teaching function of the university library* (*The universities review*, February 1958).

HUMPHREYS, K W: *Standing Conference on National and University Libraries* (*Libri*, 1956, 1962).

HUMPHREYS, K W: *The subject specialist in national and university libraries* (*Libri*, 1967).

HUNT, C J: *A computerised acquisitions system in Manchester University Library* (*Program*, July 1971).

KELLER, J E: *Program budgeting and cost benefit analysis in libraries* (*College and research libraries*, March 1969).

KILGOUR, F G: *The economic goal of library automation* (*College and research libraries*, July 1969).

LANCOUR, H: *Training for librarianship in North America* (*Library Association record*, September 1951).

LINE, M B: *Staffing university libraries* (*British universities annual*, 1965).

LINE, M B and BRYANT, P: *How golden is your retriever?* (*Library Association record*, May 1969).

MARSH, A S: *The library in the university hall of residence* (*Library Association record*, May 1959).

MEWS, H: *Library instruction to students at the University of Reading* (*Education libraries bulletin*, Summer 1968).

MUNN, R F: *The bottomless pit, or the academic library as viewed from the Administration Building* (*College and research libraries*, January 1968).

PAFFORD, J H P: *Book selection in the university library* (UNESCO *Bulletin*, January-February 1963).

R, J M: *The new climax to the Glasgow skyline* (*Architectural review*, April 1969).

RATCLIFFE, F W: *Problems of open access in large academic libraries* (*Libri*, 1968).

SEYMOUR, C A: *Weeding the collection: a review of research on identifying obsolete stock. Part I: Monographs. Part II: Serials* (*Libri*, 1972).

SHAW, C M: *Duplicate provision for undergraduates* (*Journal of librarianship*, July 1971).

STEVENS, R E: *The microform revolution* (*Library trends*, January 1971).

STEVENSON, C L and COOPER, J A: *A computerised accounts system at the City University* (*Program*, April 1968).

TAYLOR, L E: *The challenge of automation for the established university library* (*South African libraries*, January 1969).

THOMPSON, J: *Book classification in new university libraries* (*Library Association record*, September 1963).

THOMPSON, J: *Book selection in a university library* (In *From publisher to reader*. London, Library Association, London and Home Counties Branch, 1972).

THOMPSON, J: *Revision of stock in academic libraries* (*Library Association record*, March 1973).

URQUHART, D J: *The National Lending Library, 1968* (*Library Association record*, March 1969).

WELLS, A J: *Shared cataloguing: a new look at an old problem* (ASLIB *Proceedings*, December 1968).

WYATT, R W P: *Producing a serials catalogue on tape* (*Library Association record*, July 1969).

INDEX

Staff—*contd*

  structure, 37-39

  training, 48-49

Staff manuals, 46-47, 82

Staff meetings, 47-48

Standing Conference of National and University Libraries, 153-154

Standing Conference on Library Materials on Africa, 148

Stock—

  categories of material, 51-54

  little-used materials, 64-69

  selection, 74-77

  size, 77-78

  special collections, 69-73

Stocktaking, 104-105

Storage centres, 66-69

Students—

  book provision, 21, 54-57

Subject catalogues, 96-97

Subject specialization, 38-39, 113-118

Sub-librarians, 35

Tables, 135

Telex, 145

Undergraduate collections, *see* Students—book provision

Undergraduates, *see* Students

Universal Decimal Classification, 99-100

University, College and Research Section (Library Association), 153

University government, 13-14

University Grants Committee, 9-10, 17

University librarian, *see* Librarian

University of London Library Depository, 68

Ventilation, *see* Air-conditioning